Walter C. Smith

A Heretic

And other poems

Walter C. Smith

A Heretic
And other poems

ISBN/EAN: 9783337006556

Printed in Europe, USA, Canada, Australia, Japan

Cover: Foto ©Thomas Meinert / pixelio.de

More available books at **www.hansebooks.com**

A HERETIC AND OTHER POEMS

BY THE AUTHOR OF "OLRIG GRANGE," "HILDA," "KILDROSTAN,"
"NORTH COUNTRY FOLK," ETC.

PUBLISHED BY

JAMES MACLEHOSE AND SONS, GLASGOW,

Publishers to the University.

MACMILLAN AND CO., LONDON AND NEW YORK.

London, - - - - *Simpkin, Marshall, Hamilton, Kent and Co., Limited.*
Cambridge, - - - *Macmillan and Bowes.*
Edinburgh, - - *Douglas and Foulis.*

MDCCCXCI.

A HERETIC

AND OTHER POEMS

BY
WALTER C. SMITH

Glasgow
JAMES MACLEHOSE & SONS
PUBLISHERS TO THE UNIVERSITY

1891

All rights reserved

CONTENTS.

	PAGE
A HERETIC,	1
SABBATH EVENING LONG AGO,	34
CREEDS,	38
THE DISCOVERY OF GOD,	42
THE INVENTION OF GOD,	48
THE VISION OF GOD,	52
THE BURDEN OF GOD,	55
WHAT PILATE THOUGHT OF IT,	65
A PULPITEER,	90
RUGGLES, THE SALVATIONIST,	125
HERR PROFESSOR KUPFER-NICKEL,	135
A DREAM,	150
MORAL-SUBLIME,	164
MIRREN,	173
A DARK EVENING,	188
FOUND AND LOST,	190

THE LETTRE DE CACHET,

A CALM,

SPRING MORNING,

ORWELL,

PAUL IN TARSUS,

A Heretic.

YES, he was there at the grave, and we
   Eyed each other with meaning look,
Wondering what he had come to see;
Yet we pitied him, too, ere long, as he
   Stood by himself alone, and shook
While the earth fell dull on the coffin lid.
But why had he come where he was not bid?
He might have known he would mar our meeting,
   Who neither its love nor its grief could share.
And how could we give him a word of greeting?—
   He! the last man that we looked for there.

So, lonely and silent he took his place,
    And silent and lonely he went his way.
But what was the shadow that lay on his face?
Was it, maybe, some touch of the tender grace,
    And the lingering love of a former day?
It puzzled me then; but I let him go
Lonely away, with his head bent low.

They had been friends in youth, had read
Together the words of the classic dead—
Epic and drama and lyric bold,
    And sage discourse of the wise and true,
And the fabled tale, and the legend old
    Where the faiths of a rank religion grew;
And many a close-writ notebook told
    How well the past life of the world they knew,
How much of the gods and the wits of Greece,
And of Rome with its arts of war and peace.

Oft wandering, too, by brake and brook,
  Or seated on lichened boulder stone,
They read as in an open book
  How earth was fashioned, and rocks had grown,
By frost and ice, by fire and flood,
From the weltering slime of the primal mud;
And what the records of nature bore
Of the struggle of Life from less to more—
What mosses in the swamps grew rank,
  What fishes stirred the long sea-weeds,
What great beasts on the river's bank
  Went crashing through the giant reeds.
So had they searched, through ages vast,
The strange grave-yards of the buried Past.

Later, their converse had mostly been
  With Fathers and Schoolmen and knotty Creeds,
And Councils, where subtlest wits were seen
  Busily sowing the fruitful seeds

Of faith and doubt, and love and hate,
And all that chequers our mortal fate.
The fall too of Empire, the dark sunset
  Of learning through lust of power and gold,
The mighty Popes, and the mightier yet
  Who wrought reform in the days of old,
And martyr-sorrows by fire and cord,
And the glory and triumph of God's pure Word,
These, too, they pondered, laying up store
Of late born science and old world lore.
So had the Kirk for her sons designed
That the rich in faith should be full in mind.

Then settled near each other—this,
In a rural parish of easy bliss,
That, in a neighbouring city rife
With the questionings of a keen young life—
They walked together side by side,
And each of the other would speak with pride:

How one had treasures of learning vast,
And one had thoughts that were sure to cast
A larger light upon life and death,
And gird up the loins of our dwindling faith.
Brothers first in the toils of youth,
Brothers now in the bonds of truth,
Each in the other was fain to see
The powers of the world that was to be.

But one man like a tree shall stand,
   Leafing and fruiting year by year,
And cling to his little patch of land,
   And cast a shade for the lazy steer,
With no more change than the passing breeze
   Makes when it tosses the creaking bough;
And prosperous, plentiful, full of ease,
   To-morrow he shall be the same as now.
Another shall flow like a freshening stream,
   Flashing there where the sunbeam flies,

Eddying here in a brooding dream,
  And all its life in its movement lies;
This the law of his being strange,
Ever he grows by flux and change.
What would you? Nature will have her way;
Will mend by night what you mar by day,
And laugh at the man who would say her
  Nay.
Tree cannot pluck up its roots and go,
Restless stream cannot cease to flow,
Each must obey the high Law given
To the things of earth by the Lord of Heaven.

And some read many books, and grow
Wiser and better by all they know;
From·thoughts of other men their own
Get warmth and colour and richer tone,
And what is old they make as new
From the shaping mind it passes through:

It was but a seed when it was sown,
But a goodly plant in their souls has grown,
For all that they gather with patient strife
Is penetrated with mystic life.
Another shall read and heap up lore,
Yet be no wiser than ever before;
Folios mighty he knows by rote,
   And each edition, its date, and size,
Page and paragraph well can quote,
   And where a word on the margin lies;
Hardly a question up shall spring,
Sudden as startled bird on wing,
But a loaded gun is up to sight
With a score of quotations to settle it right;
Yet never a thought of his own has he,
Nor any mind but memory.

So these twain took their several ways,
Though each was full of the other's praise,

Keeping ever a constant heart,
While drifting more and more wide apart.
For he whom we laid in the grave that day,—
 Honoured and wept for his service—learned
By change and sorrow the sacred way
 Which the dull, slow book-worm never discerned.

He had come among us in brilliant youth,
 Eloquent, earnest, eager to tell
Just the old story we held for truth,
 And we praised him for it, and liked him well;
Praised the round periods shaped with care,
And the brilliant tropes that he did not spare,
And liked the man and his modest air.
Praised him and liked him! What would he
 more?
Welcome his knock at the cottage door,
Welcome at school to the children gay,
 Welcome his presence at wedding feast,

Welcome where sickness restless lay,
  Welcome as Comforter, Prophet and Priest—
What would he more than already he had?
And why should his countenance now be sad?

Say you are set to pasture sheep,
  Taught where the short, sweet grasses grow,
And the tender ewes and the lambs to keep
  From the wily fox and the hooded crow,
And how to shift them from hill to dale,
And how to bring healing to them that ail,
And when to fold them, and feed them well
While the snow lies deep upon field and fell.
And so you tend them with care, and they
  Trust your shepherding, as you strive
To keep them safe in the good old way—
  But somehow or other they do not thrive;
They do not grow as they ought to grow,
But pine where the quiet waters flow,

And many are ailing, and none grow fat—
Could you be well content with that?
Nay, you are not there to be liked and praised,
But to see that the sheep are fitly grazed.

Or say that you go a-fishing, well
   Equipt with a handy rod and reel,
And the temptingest flies that ever fell,
   Like light, where the rippling waters steal,
And you know all the likely casts and pools,
And to ply your art by the latest rules.
Could you be satisfied now to see
   Shoals come sniffing about your hooks,
As it were a pleasure for them to be
   Playing there, in the shining brooks,
With the golden wings and the scarlet dyes
Of all those beautiful summer flies,
If never a speckled trout would touch
The dainty things that they liked so much?

Greatly our Shepherd, then, we admired,
   And greatly his fishing-craft we praised;
But that was not what his heart desired,
   And therefore with sorrowing eyes he gazed
Round and down on the thronging pews,
As one who had failed in telling his news.
For our life went on as it did before,
Heaping up treasures from less to more,
Seeking our pleasure, and serving our sins,
And giving our honours to him that wins.

And so he began to ask, "What next?
   Can I spend my years on a fruitless task?
My soul is weary and sore perplexed,
   Will God not give me the boon I ask?
Better go plough a straight furrow, and reap,
Better the broom of a crossing sweep,
Labour of any kind one can see
Good coming out of, than this for me."

Some would have laid all the blame on the flock,
And called their hearts hard as a flinty rock;
But that was never his way; for he
    Searched himself and his work to find
What might the cause of his failure be,
    And whether it were in his heart or mind.
Was it the good news of God he had spoken?
Was it the true Bread of life he had broken?
And the Christ he had preached, was He God's own Son?
Or only the Christ whom the schoolmen spun,
Part of the earth, and part of the air,
From the small fine threads of their logic bare?

Now came a season of deep unrest,
    Of teaching thought to be lame and halt,
And meetings of elders with minds oppressed,
    And meddling of ministers finding fault.

For the fight he was fighting all the week through,
As the Sabbath came round, he must fight it anew;
And now it went this way, now it went that,
Till we hardly could tell what he meant to be at;
But we felt he was real, and groping about
In search of a Faith that he had to find out.
Slowly the light came; slowly it grew,
Not without questionings, Could it be true?
And faint heart-misgivings, What might be the end?
Must he lose for the sake of it lover and friend?
Sometimes resisting it when it seemed clearest,
Sometimes afraid of it when it felt dearest,
Sometimes persuaded it could not be right,
Else the saints nearest God would have glowed in
    its light,
And sometimes defiant and scornful, he,
As one who knew what the cost must be,
Hurled it at us, and went his way,
To kneel in his closet, and weep and pray.

But he settled at last in the lucent calm
Of a restful faith which was sweet as a Psalm—
Calm and sweet as the waters blest
Where the Good Shepherd causeth His flock to rest.

At first we heard him with growing fear.
   Was he hitting indeed at our cherished beliefs?
Was he sapping the truth to our fathers dear?
   Was he shooting heretical arrows in sheafs?
Was he driving shafts through the Catechism
To undermine our old Calvinism?
Some held it was only the truth he sought,
Truth which at any price must be bought:
And some, that he ne'er should have come to preach
If he had not already the truth to teach.
And so, at each fireside the battle raged
Which he with himself in anguish waged,
And we searched the Book, and we gathered store
   Of other books, and we deemed them good,

Not for the wealth of their learned lore,
But for help that they gave us in living more
   Nobly and truly as Christians should;
That was his test for every thought,
Will it lift you up nearer to God or not?

O that was a spring time of sowing seed—
   Seed of the better life surely—for mind
Was quickened by him, and the soul was freed
   From dead traditions that bind and blind;
It was a time too of tears and prayers,
   And bearing of crosses by high and low;
If the enemy also sowed his tares,
   He warned us well that it must be so.
In the end, when his way at length was clear,
   And the light shone quietly forth in power,
And he came to us speaking good words of good
     cheer
   That dropt on our souls like a summer shower,

How we waited for Sunday then, eager to listen
To a message that made the heart glow, and eye glisten!
O the hush of the multitude, breathless and still,
As their souls bowed before him, and moved at his will!

Meanwhile his friend in his rural home
Read many a clasped, white-vellumed tome,
Black-lettered, and with red-edged leaf,
And never a sentence clear and brief.
Meikle he read, but little he grew;
   A dwarf in giant's armour he;
And all that was old he held for true,
   And all that was new must error be;
Fresh lights indeed on the earth might shine,
But nothing fresh upon things divine;
And little he heeded the voice which said,
I am living, and these are dead.

Then some came to him, whispering, "Lo!
The hour is come, and the man we know.
The friend of thy youth has gone astray
From the beaten path of the narrow way,
And leadeth others to do likewise,
 As there are always silly sheep
Will follow the bell-wether, when he tries
 O'er his own shadow in vain to leap.
That which the Fathers held for truth
In the faith-sure days of the church's youth,
That which Divines at a later stage,
With the learning ripe of a thoughtful age,
Fashioned into a Creed compact,
Every link of it strong as fact,
Every joint of it fitting tight
As Scripture and Reason could shape them
 right—
That, like another blind Samson, he,
 Making sport for the Philistine,

Would fain pull down on our heads, that we
    May die like the Gadarene herd of swine:
(Figures are apt to get confused,
In the heat of angry passion used.)
But now is the harvest come at last
    Of all thy sowing of fruitless seed;
God has been guiding thee in the past
    To help His Church in her hour of need.
He is thy friend, and dear to thee,
But not so dear as the Truth should be;
Up, then, and gird thine armour on,
Or take thy sling and the pebble stone,
And smite this giant of carnal doubt.
The Church must deal with him; but without
The lore of the ages, known to thee,
Hardly her way shall be plain to see;
For the critical, carping spirit abroad
    Lies ever in wait for the Church's tripping,
If she miss but a turn of the changing road,

Or a chance wrong word from her mouth come
   slipping,
And they scoff and mock, and fleer and flout
If a date be wrong, or a jot left out.
Heaven trained thee for this task. Behold,
There is glory to win, and maybe—gold,
When the true champion of the faith
Has stricken this heresy unto death."

They were not many-thoughted men,
   Nor wise at winning souls, but yet
Fitly and well they reasoned then
   To snare this soul in their wily net,
For he in his heart was vain and cold,
And hankered, too, with the lust of gold;
And this was how the leaven wrought
As he sat him down by the fire, and thought—
"How can I do it? He is my friend,
   Tender and true, and a saintly spirit,

Living, by work and prayer, to mend
  The ills and woes that we all inherit.
They'll call me a Balaam, a Judas,—what not?
If I meddle with that which concerns me not.
But I will not prophesy at their call;
And the profits, if any, must needs be small.
Yet should not a warning word be spoken,
Even at the risk of a friendship broken?
Can I in faithfulness let him go
  Unrebuked in his erring way,
Marring the ancient doctrine so,
  And leading others, too, far astray?
'Tis pleasant to find my work at last
  Appreciated as it should be;
And what, if, indeed, through the busy Past,
  God for this has been training me?
So they read it, as men of sense,
Skilled in the ways of Providence.
It is right to do what the Church requires,

And to tend the flame of her altar fires,
And glory is good, and likewise gold,
When the lambs are many within the fold.
How painful soever, then, I must speak;—
And, besides, he is clearly all wrong in his Greek."

Followed a sharp Remonstrance, charged
With high authorities, and enlarged
With customary polemic hits—
The shallow trick of barren wits—
As "love of novelty—fickle mind—
   Failure of logic, if beauty of art—
Hunger for fame of the emptiest kind—
   Itch of vanity in the heart—
Knowledge that had not a touch of grace,
Not accurate either, and out of place."
You know the style; it was commoner once
Than it is to-day, when the learned dunce
Is of little account. As he read the "proof,"

Though he knew how unkindly his words must seem,
Like a pigeon perched on the high house-roof,
He crooned and swelled in a vain fond dream
Of all the honours that he should win,
When scholars his learned volume read,
And the wealth of coin that it might bring in,
And the name that should live when he was dead;
But he did not remember the love he lost—
The broken seal of the Holy Ghost.
One word only he spoke out plain,
But that word measured the bulk of his brain:
"That Aorist, now; he is clearly wrong;
I have touched him there, and my point is strong."
For the faith and the hope of men, he wist,
All hinged on the turn of an Aorist.

Remonstrance led to Rejoinder, of course,
Deftly handled with point and force,

And equal learning and dainty wit,
And there was not an unkind word in it.
"Pleasant," he writ, "was a quiet life
    Spent among big-margined folio books,
Far from the town with its busy strife,
    'Mid the singing of larks, and the cawing of rooks;
And well for his friend to have lettered ease,
    For the Church to have scholars ripe and good,
Though it is not for any themselves to please,
    And sit in brown study, and dream and brood,
Fighting the battles of long ago
With ghosts that are wandering to and fro,
When they ought of rights to be lying low.
For himself, his task had been plainly set
Where the eager throng in the market met,
And the rush of thoughts into men's vexed minds
Was borne like the dust on the wild March winds,

And would not be settled by tense or mood,
Or aught that the nice grammarian could.
He must serve his time, for he did not think
    God had mistaken the time of day,
And sent him forth, like an owl to blink
    At noon, instead of the evening grey;
But to look in the face of man, and see
    What was aching his heart and brow,
And where the shadow of Mystery
    Lay on the face of the dial now.

"Fresh lights had shone upon earth and heaven,
And time had his ancient secrets given
Up to our search from the earth and stone
That held the story of Babylon.
Not now could any one wholly read
The truth aright, if he gave no heed
To that which the Fathers could not know--
The lights which out of the ages grow.

And ere the brief hours of his day were run,
He would like to feel that his task was done
With clear intelligence of the time,
    Wasting nothing on mere by-play,
But filling his place in the plan sublime
    God worked out in His own great way.
Others might come to mend it soon,
    To-morrow a different work might need,
Men must change with the changing moon,
And life be sung to another tune,
    And shape itself to a larger Creed.
Faith in God was the only way,
And there was no last word on that to say.

"What have I done? I have only told
    My flock of the boundless love of God,
Which is not straitened, but doth enfold
    All that on earth have their abode,
All in the Universe that dwell

In the heights of heaven, or the depths of hell;
For there is no shore where that ocean breaks
    And finds its limit: God is not there
Where Love is not, that our burden takes;
    But God is love, and is everywhere.
And I told them, that God and His grace and work
    Are not tied fast to a Bishop's crook,
Are not shut up in an ordered kirk,
    Nor yet bound up in a printed book,
For all good thoughts that visited them,
    All longings for the pure and true,
All from His inspiration came;
    And there was not an erring soul but knew
The pleading tones of the Father's love
Calling—calling him from above.
And I taught moreover that they who hear,
    And turn from the evil of their ways,
Shall find that His mercy is ever near,
    And sing to Him yet in a song of praise;

For among the living, among the dead,
   Yesterday, to-day, and for ever,
He is still the same, as the Spirit said,
   Pouring forth love as a flowing river.
Is it heresy to have taught them so?
   I glory in it, and ever must,
Ever with Christ my faith must go,
   When He seeks the living to make them just,
   Or joins the dead where they lie in dust;
For He must be doing His Father's will,
Bearing the message of mercy still."

Process of heresy then began,
   And who but his ancient friend was fit,
Since the heretic too was a learned man,
   With competent knowledge to handle it?
O they were grieved, for well they wot
   The man was good, and the work he did,
A saintly spirit in deed and thought,

Though he plainly taught what the Church forbid:
But never a heresy yet had thriven
But what some holy man had given
A tone to it that appeared from Heaven.
It was all the worse for the Church, they said,
    When a man of God from the old paths broke;
But there was little to fear or dread,
    When the heretic was like other folk.

Weekly they met in hot debate,
    And weekly they preached on the business too,
Daily also, and early and late,
    We all debated the case anew.
Never such stir was known in the place;
    Never such searching of chapter and verse;
Never such talk of election and grace,
    Never such arguments clear and terse;
Never such stores of theology brought
    From hiding places in old men's heads,

Never such troubled and anxious thought,
    As we walked by the way, or lay still in our beds,
To think of the man that we held so dear
    Badgered as if he were fool or rogue:
But at length, in the cold dark end of the year,
    They cast him out of their synagogue.

I was there on that chill December night
    When they gave their verdict, and spake his doom
By a single candle's glimmering light
    That was only just seen in the dusky gloom.
Many were weeping, and some men swore,
    But a low laugh rose when the light died out,
And we said, "Here we seek for the truth no more,
    They have left us in darkness to wander about."
Yet were we glad that the end had come,
    And the torrents of foolishest speech were dumb.

But in the name of God to smite

Him that was walking with God in light!
And in the name of God to wreak
Wrath on the lowly heart and meek!
And in the name of God to pray
O'er such a work as they did that day,
Little witting what they were at!—
In God's name what is the end of that?

Outcast now from its fellowship,
   Still to the Kirk he fondly clung,
And often he said, with quivering lip,
   How good it was, when the bell was rung,
   To go where the grand old Psalms were sung,
And to be where lowly hearts were bent
In prayer or holy Sacrament;
For the Kirk made brave and earnest men,
And he loved her now as he loved her then.
So he lived on, the meekest saint,
Nor wasted his life in vain complaint,

Nor formed another sect to claim
That it was the true Jerusalem,
And rear its altars in his name;
But gathered around him thoughtful youth,
Inspiring them with the love of truth,
And to look for guidance from above,
And to believe that God is Love.

At first, of course, we were only few—
   Just one here, and another there—
Suspected and distrusted too,
   And work was scanty, and calls were rare.
But soon the leaven spread, and we
Became a goodly company:
And many a pulpit in the land
   Ere long was quickened by his faith,
And sounded forth the message grand
   That Love had vanquished sin and death,
That God had been a little child,

And walked with sinners, undefiled,
And with the wicked had made His grave,
    That grace and hope might come to all,
And all might join the battle brave
    Who heard and would obey His call.
And we grew bold, and dared to greet
    The outcast in his failing years
With words of love and honour meet
    That filled his wistful eyes with tears—
Never a task I laboured at
So much to my liking as writing that—
For he had meekly borne the yoke,
    And now behold the seed had sprung,
And over all the Church awoke
    The same glad strain which he had sung.
O mystery of truth, whose hour
Of sorrow is its day of power,
Which but accepts its Cross, and then
Rides forth in its might to conquer men!

But who was the heretic kept apart
From the truth and life by his faithless heart?
He who was loser, but still loved on?
Or he who gave up his love, and won?
Ah! would you read God's meaning? look
Not on the bright, shining page of His Book,
But where the shadow lies dark on the face
Of some tragic failure, some proud disgrace.
For the loss is gain, and the gain is loss,
  And the shame is glory when He wills
That thou shouldst shine in the healing Cross,
  Which all the Law by love fulfils.

Sabbath Evening Long Ago.

I see the old home on the Sabbath night—
    It smelt of heresy to call it Sunday,
A heathen name, although we held it right
    To paganize the Saturday and Monday.

The cruise hung on the jamb, with poor rush pith
    That, soaked in whale oil, dimly kept a-gleaming;
More shadows filled the room than lights therewith,
    And how those wavering shadows set me dreaming!

A sea-coal fire glowed on the old Dutch slates,
    And on the brown carved settle near the doorway,
And on a rack of willow-pattern plates,
    And on a bronze-hued wooden bowl from Norway.

A mighty cauldron simmered by the fire,
    Whereto our hungry eyes kept often turning,
For the much-preaching sharpened the desire
    To satisfy the flesh we had been spurning.

In the big chair the father gravely sat,
    And round the fire the household gathered quiet;
The dog wheeled round, and, coiling on the mat,
    Slept through the lesson, profiting not by it.

And then we went right through the "Catechism,"
    From "Man's chief end" to "Amen" in conclusion —
Heaven's white light broken in a logic prism
    To clear our thought, and end in dire confusion.

Mostly I did not understand at all,
    And my mind wandered off to hear the shouting
Of comrades at a game of bat or ball;
    But where I understood, it set me doubting.

So those high orthodoxies came to be
　　Quick seeds in me of heterodox opinion,
And ere I wist, my thoughts were all at sea,
　　And drifted, holden by no wise dominion.

I knew not how those Westminster Divines
　　To Scots beyond the Tweed their faith had given,
But I rebelled to travel on those lines
　　Which made so hard and dark a way to Heaven.

Still the small mind chafed at the strenuous thought
　　Of those stern Puritans who faced, unwincing,
The darkest problems of our human lot,
　　And solved them with a text, as all-convincing.

But while the grave old father questioned on,
　　I marked his dome of forehead, time had wrinkled,
And to myself I kept my thoughts alone, [twinkled.
　　And the dog dreamed on, and the rushlight

In him there was a faith serene and strong,
    In me an unrest, like the rush of water;
Without, there was a Credo hard and long,
    Within, there was a resolute Negatur.

Yet in his stern creed lay a tender heart,
    That husk o'erlaid a wealth of human kindness
And love, that fain their wisdom would impart
    To purge the young soul of its earthly blindness.

And it did store the mind with furniture—
    In forms antique, forbidding peaceful slumber,
But morticed well, and fashioned to endure,
    Hard to get into, or out of heads they cumber.

I wot not what our later faiths may do
    For us, what time our troubled lives may need them,
But through that stern old creed a nation grew
    Toughest and staunchest in the fight of freedom.

Creeds.

Ah! these old creeds
Who can believe them to-day?
Yet were brave deeds
Inspired by them once, too; and they
   Made men of heroic mould
   In the great fighting ages of old.

Is it the wounds
Which science has given? or the sap
   On critical grounds,
Which has brought about their mishap?
   Nay, these touched not a vital spot,
   Though they brag of the wreck they have wrought.

But the spirit has risen
From the hard, narrow letter which kept
   Men's thoughts in a prison,
Where they struggled or languished or slept;
     And now we can soar high above
     All the creeds but the Credo of Love.

   They are things of the past,
Survivals, and now out of date;
   The men were not cast
In our moulds, who endured such a weight,
     So linked and compact: let them go,
     They who wore them had no room to grow.

   All too complete,
They were subtly and skilfully wrought
   With logic neat;
But they are not in touch with our thought;
     And they will not allow they have found
     Any spot where they have not sure ground.

They are ever so far
From the days we are living in now,
From our work and our war,
And the thoughts that are aching our brow;
And yet though they be but part true,
Vain to patch up the old, or make new.

Creed-making now
In these latter ages of time
Would yield stuff, I trow,
Thin and loose as a small poet's rhyme—
Tags and thrums, hints and guesses, no more,
With a deep, settled doubt at the core.

What not to believe,
That now is the stage we are at;
And how shall we weave
Any faith to live on out of that?
There must go to the making of creeds
Sure hearts, girded up for high deeds.

CREEDS

But ours is an age
Of unmaking, taking things down :
  For the warfare we wage
We must swarm from the fortified town,
    And spread out to find air and room
    Beyond the old walls and their gloom.

Yet we have faith
In the Right and the True and the Good,
  And in Him whose last breath
Was the prayer of a pitiful mood,
    Which smites the meek spirit with awe,
    And with Love, the true life of all Law.

The Discovery of God.

WHO was the man that found out God?
   And what the method that he took?
   Did he with patient travail look
For footprints on the sand or sod,

Making it plain that, on a time,
   A mighty architect stood here
   Building the earth up, tier on tier,
And working out a plan sublime?

Or did he trace, with curious skill,
   Nice-fashioning touches on the clay
   That man was made of, and the way
That it was modelled to fulfil

The artist's purpose, when at length
    The pulses of its life should beat,
    And find the eye and ear complete,
And hand with delicate touch and strength?

And as he traced the facts and laws,
    Close-linking the high argument
    Of reason, was the great event—
An infinite all-designing Cause?

Thus, step by step, did he go on,
    Groping through darkness toward light,
    Until the vision of glory bright
Dawned on his soul, and doubt was gone,

And in the splendour of the day
    The universe revealed its sense,
    And throbbed with clear intelligence,
And bade him worship now and pray,

For lo! the wondrous Book, no more
    Anonymous, disclosed to view
    Its Author and its meaning too,
Which were a secret heretofore?

Ah! what a moment that had been,
    When such a thought first broke on him,
    And filled his being to the brim
With awe of what his mind had seen!

Who was the grand discoverer?
    What age was honoured to contain
    This man of subtle and daring brain—
The one divine philosopher?

Could mortals e'er forget his name,
    Or history fail to note the day
    When that dread veil was rent away,
And God a proven Truth became?

One finds a new world, one, a star
    Undreamt of hitherto, and men
    Hold high their names in honour then
Through all the ages near and far.

But what are these to him who found
    The truth in which all others meet,
    The central thought which makes complete,
And clears up all the glorious round,

The will which shapes what may befall,
    The power that wrought whate'er hath been,
    The light wherein all light is seen,
The life that is the life of all?

Nay, no Columbus here may boast
    That, plunging in an unknown sea,
    He made this grand discovery,
Being sore-spent and tempest-tossed.

No seeker sought, till he did find
   The secret hid from ages past,
   The mystery of the First and Last,
The Peace that filleth heart and mind,

By links of patient reason brought
   Out of the sum of finite things.
   He reasons ill whose reason brings
Such outcome from his partial thought—

From light and shadow perfect light,
   Pure good from mingled good and ill,
   From tokens of mechanic skill
Illimitable glory and might.

Vain dreamer of an idle dream
   In logic forms! Did any one
   Discover by his quest the sun,
That seeks us with his searching beam?

THE DISCOVERY OF GOD.

Who pries about the world to find
    Proof that he is in heaven? who mines
    The earth in search of frequent signs
That shall suffice to clear his mind,

And certify the wondrous power,
    That burns upon the morning cloud,
    And makes the song-bird glad and loud,
And paints the shining leaf and flower?

Thou did'st not find God hidden there
    In problem of his acts and days;
    But He reveals himself, and lays
To the pure heart his glory bare.

The Invention of God.

Some tell us that, in evil hour,
   Our fears invented God, the dread
   Of our forefathers lying dead,
Or of some dark, malignant Power

That sendeth pestilence and drought,
   And storms and desolating wars,
   And horrid glare of baleful stars,
And grief and pain, and fear and doubt:

Wherefore the troubled spirit dreamed
   A Phantom stood upon its path,
   And hastened to appease his wrath
By whatsoe'er it most esteemed.

THE INVENTION OF GOD.

Man did not know the law that binds
   Whatever is with all that was,
   And in the sum of complex cause
A deep unconscious wisdom finds.

A savage without science, he
   Sat shivering in his dirty rag,
   And deemed some godhead held a bag
Filled full of pain and misery,

Which he let loose on hapless men,
   What time, an hungered, he would dine
   On ample flesh, and bread, and wine,
And found his altar stinted then.

And so man's fear invented God;
   For thunder-clap and stormy blast,
   And fire-stream from the mountain cast
Seemed the fell strokes of his angry rod;

And pestilence his deadly breath,
 And war a game he loved to play
 For pastime of an idle day,
That gambled with our life and death:

Wherefore men crept up to his feet,
 And licked the dust in abject fear,
 And howled their prayers into his ear,
Or gashed them, and their bosoms beat.

Strange savage, in the nutting wood,
 Who, just emerged from apehood, framed
 Articulate speech, and all things named,
And brooding in a troubled mood,

Invented God! Our triumphs are
 But trifles it were best to hide,
 But poor mechanic toys beside
The trophies of thy fruitful war.

O semi-brute ! thou had'st a dream
    Transcending all that we can reach,
    For thou invented'st God and Speech,
And we have only compassed—Steam.

And Thou dark Phantom of our fears,
    How comes the heart to cling to Thee
    For comfort in its misery,
And drying of its blinding tears?

The stream that from the height comes down
    And foams along the rock-strewn course,
    Can never rise above its source,
But creepeth down by grange and town ;

Yet from that spring of coward dread,
    That phantom born of wrath and death,
    Come holy love, brave-hearted faith,
And hope with heavenly visions fed !

The Vision of God.

O THE silences of heaven,
    How they speak to me of God,
Now the veil in twain is riven
    That concealed where He abode!
Yet its clouds were once around Him,
    And I sought Him in despair,
And never there I found Him,
    Till I brought Him with me there.

Not the optic glass revealed Him,
    No mechanical device
Pierced the darkness that concealed Him
    With a vision more precise:

Only lowliness can merit
    That His secret He should tell;
Only spirit seeth spirit,
    And the heart that loveth well.

Never till His love hath found thee,
    Shall the cloud and mist depart;
Vain to seek Him all around thee,
    Till He dwell within thy heart.
Not without thee, but within thee
    Must the oracle be heard,
As He seeketh still to win thee,
    And to guide thee by His word.

When I found Him in my bosom,
    Then I found Him everywhere,
In the bud and in the blossom,
    In the earth and in the air;

And He spake to me with clearness
From the silent stars that say,
As ye find Him in His nearness,
Ye shall find Him far away.

The Burden of God.

I BORE a load of doubt and care,
   And could not reason it away;
It might have no right to be there,
   Yet clung to me by night and day.
And I was fain to be alone,
   A stranger in a far off land,
Where friend and helper I had none,
   Nor any that could understand.
O for a glad, entrancing faith!
   O for an all-controlling thought
To fill my soul, as with a breath
   That from the Eternal life is brought!
Let me but be alone with God
   A little while on some high place,

Where rarely foot of man hath trod,
    That I may see Him face to face.
So did they long of old, who built
    High altars on the hill-tops bare,
To leave their load of sin and guilt,
    And find the peace they hoped for there.

Then I went toiling up the glen,
    Like one that wanders in a dream,
Past broad-eaved homes of toiling men,
    Along the swiftly rushing stream,
Past the white kirk with ruddy spire,
    And solitary wayside shrine,
Where peasant mothers did admire
    The mother of the Babe divine,
Past orchards where the tawny steer,
    Black-muzzled, stood and whisked his tail,
While men sat in the tavern near,
    With flask of wine or mug of ale.

I heard the sharp *whish* of the scythe,
    And dragging of the patient rake,
I heard the children singing blithe,
    And felt as if my heart would break.
They sang the song of Bethlehem,
    And glad their voices were and clear;
And oh that I could sing like them,
    And only knew that God would hear !

Still on, I bore my burden on,
    Finding no help in kirk or shrine,
Or crucifix of carven stone,
    Or picture of the babe divine :
Alone, I must be all alone,
    Beyond the mighty wooded slopes ;
I would have company with none,
    But those vast, silent mountain tops
Which held me with their snowy spell,
    And bade me come to where they stood,

And in their white robes worshipped well
    The Everlasting Pure and Good.

I took the steep rock-path that winds
    Through the pine wood above the stream,—
High up the grey-green glacier grinds,
    Far down its grey-green waters gleam,
A torrent from a neighbouring cliff
    Leaped down, and disappeared half way,
To fall in tremulous mist, as if
    Nature to me was fain to say—
See how the rush of lofty thought,
    The higher that its way appears,
The deeper that its rest is sought,
    Still vanishes in mist and tears.

Still up the rugged path I went,
    With panting breath and trembling knees,
And weary limb, and back low bent,
    Till, past the belt of great pine trees,

I came upon a sunny glade
    Open and green, with brooks and wells,
And crocus fields where cattle wade,
    With noise of many jangling bells,
And flat-roofed chalets, piled with stone,
    For winds are boisterous there and wild,
But kirk or steeple there was none,
    Only the Virgin and her Child,
Kept in some homely box for shrine,
    And sheltered in a quiet nook,
Where humble worship might incline
    With bended knee and lowly look.
But all these fond traditions stood—
    How sweet soe'er their tender grace—
Between me and the Pure and Good,
    And I must see Him face to face.

A little speech, a little rest,
    A cup of goat's milk at the door;

Bid me not stay and be your guest,
    There are a good eight hours and more,
Before the sun dips in the west,
    And I must on at any price,
To see his evening glories rest
    Upon the pale green glacier ice,
And on the web of pallid snow,
    That wraps the hills in raiment white,
And on the changing clouds below,
    That catch the fringes of His light.
I did not tell my inmost thought:
    Those neat-herds could not well divine
How I, in search of God, was brought
    Away from kirk and cross and shrine.

Still up and up; the Alpen-stock
    Oft buried in the turf before,
Now smote upon the living rock,
    And from its heart the fire-spark tore;

THE BURDEN OF GOD.

And as I trod the gradual slope
   'Neath some snow-crested precipice,
And glanced round with a passing hope
   Of chamois fleet or Edelweiss,
Lo! then my step grew lightsomer,
   And cheerily I sped along,
And in the brisk and tingling air
   I could have broken into song.
And this I took for omen true,
   That I was on the way of peace,
That doubts were where the pine-woods grew
   And with the haunts of man would cease.

And so at length I trod the snow
   On the hill-top that afternoon,
And saw it in the evening glow,
   And in the sheen o' th' pallid moon,
And saw the wondrous morning dawn
   All rosy on the white-robed peaks

That, ranged like priest-forms in their lawn,
    Served through eternal holy weeks
About the altar of the Lord,
    Awful in their blanch beauty there,
Silent as if with one accord
    Wrapt in the hush of speechless prayer.
There was no sound of man or beast,
    Nor hum of bee, nor song of bird,
And more the silence seemed increased
    What time the avalanche was heard.

Once they had held me with a spell,
    And drawn me with a mystic force,
Those hills, as deeming God must dwell
    There where the waters had their source,
Which made the vales and meadows glad;
    There where in majesty sublime
The changeless snow-clad summits had
    No reckoning of the passing time.

There 'mid the everlasting snow
    Should I not see the eternal right,
And look down on the mists below,
    And gaze up to the fount of light,
And find my burden fall away,
    And feel at last the perfect calm,
That broods in the unchanging day,
    And vision of the great I Am?

But as I stood upon the height,
    I did not find what I had sought,
I did not find the perfect light,
    That answered to my wistful thought;
It did not ease me of my load,
    That I had left the world behind;
I was not any nearer God
    By being far from human kind.
And up amid the bands of ice
    And silent fields of clinging snow,

I could have purchased with a price
    The Virgin and the Babe below.
For not in nature's awfulness,
    And majesty and purity,
And not in her dread silences
    Shall God reveal His depths to thee;
But in a heart that throbs to thine,
    And tongue that speaks a human speech:
The human is the one divine,
    That yearning human souls can reach.
There is no scene of earth fulfils
    The high hope of the soaring mind,
And in the quiet of the hills
    The peace of God I did not find;
And sweet it was with weary limbs,
    Ere long to sit i' the kirk, and hear
The children singing in their hymns,
    That Christ was come, and God was near.

What Pilate Thought of It.

WHAT would you have, my Lucius? Here our wits,
Which you in Rome keep ever sharp and bright
By constant use, are blunted, and the sword
Clings to the scabbard, only to be drawn
Too late. Oh, thus and thus I should have spoken
And thus I should have done. How cleverly
We manage, when we sit down by the fire,
And, having all the dialogue to ourselves,
We find the answer pat, which does not come
I' th' strain of acting! But you do not know
This people—Would I were like you in that!
F.

"Are they dull-brained, these Jews, then? Are there
    none
To whet your wits upon, and keep them keen?
No crafty priest to fence with—demagogue
To trip up in his talk—no politic
Schemer to countermine—or wily lawyer
To follow through his trick and artifice
Of rhetoric, and exercise the brain
We used to think a good one?" Plenty of them,
Priests, plotters, demagogues as thick as flies
In Egypt, and like flies they settle on
Your eyes to sting and blind them. But they are
    not
Like other men. You cannot count upon
Their motives, or their methods, or their aims.
What they may love, and what they may abhor,
The oaths that bind them, or the gods they fear,
All are most strange and baffling. 'Tis as if
You dealt with beings of another world

Whose passions are not ours, whose ways of thinking
Are alien to our modes. The strangest people!
So pious and so wicked! methodical
In lying, with a reason always ready,
Yet full of contradictions, as the way
Of lying is apt to be even in adepts,
And they are deep practitioners. Then, too, Cæsar
Distrusts me, and when I have served him best,
Lo! comes a deputation of these Jews,
Whose women throng the backstairs of the palace,
Backed by their money-lending Trastiveres,
And every one a traitor at his heart,
Impeaching me of rapine and of blood,
And thereon comes a rescript. What can I,
But let them plot, looking as if I saw
Mere loyal service, till the plot be ripe,
Then crush them with my legions? Only force
Can rule this beastly Plebs, and their worse leaders,
And Cæsar, if he knew them as I do,

Would leave the Gauls and Britons, and let loose
The sword upon these Hebrews. Oh to be—
But for my hungry creditors—once more
I' the Campus Martius on unruliest steed,
Or scouring the Campania, rather than
Managing these cursed Jews! I've lost my nerve
Among them—yet their daughters are most fair.

But of this prophet Jesus. You must know,
I had been supping late with Rufus Naso,
And young Cornelius, and the Advocate
Publius Julius, and some other wits,
Visitors here from Rome: all full of spirits,
That hardly needed my best Cyprian wine,
Just smacking of the goatskin, to let loose
The sparkling jest, the latest story told
About the Augurs, Seneca's neat phrase,
And your quick repartee, Nerissa's strokes
Of wit, and Lydia's languishing, and all

The pleasant life about the Mammertine,
For which one longs in this Jerusalem.
This growing slack, i' th' hush we heard a song,
A great " Hal-lal " about the Temple gate,
Repeated here and there all through the town
Pleasantly, for these Jews are musical,
And have a better choir than you in Rome,
With antiphones and linked melodies
That toss the sweet strains to and fro i' th' air,
And pick them up again, and blend their notes
To catch the soul with rapture. I alone
Knew 'twas their Pascha, chief of all their Feasts,
Joyful, yet solemn, not like the wild riot
Of booths and bonfires in the Autumn when
They hold their Lupercalia, and go mad.
We had well drunk, and were in merry humour;
So nought would serve but we must travesty
The rite. By Bacchus, 'twas the rarest prank,
Though it may cost me dear. About midnight

Each girt his coat about him, donned his sandals
As ready for a journey, with a staff
Handy, for so their Priests had ordered it;
And thereupon the slaves brought in the feast.
But for a lamb we had a roasted swine,
Which is abomination to the Jew,
And sweet baked fruits instead of bitter herbs,
And flagons of rare Cyprus, and we sang
Some ribald songs to the air of their Hal-lal,
Till far into the morning. As day broke,
We heard the loud tramp of a throng of men
Fast hurrying through the streets. That sobered us.
Were those fierce Jews, then, mustering to avenge
The insult? How could I so play the fool,
Knowing the crafty Annas had his spies
About me—that they tell him all I do,
Who visits me, what letters I have writ,
Even what I eat and drink, and all my dallying
With that witch, Leila, whom I half suspect

To be the chief tale bearer? O crass fool!
To fall into his power for this poor jest.
"Ho! man the walls, draw up the guard in arms!"
Pshaw! 'tis no riot, only some mad prophet
The priests are haling to their courts. He must be
An honest one, for they'd have let him preach
Truculent lies till doomsday.

       Well; my head
Was not so clear as it had need to be
After that bout, nor were my nerves well strung,
When there rose clamorous outcry at the gate,
And I must to the Judgment Hall, where stood
A lonely prisoner, bound, and faint, and weary.
Some poor men—fishers, as I deemed, or shepherds—
Flitted about i' th' shadow, looking scared,
As loath to leave him, yet afraid to stand
Right at his side. All his accusers were
Clamouring outside the court. It would have tainted
Their sanctity at such a sacred time,

And barred them from the worship of their God,
To cross our unclean threshold; for we all—
Cæsar and all his Prætors and their courts—
Are in their eyes defiling and unholy.
They might be forging lies: no doubt, they were;
They seldom do aught else. They might embrue
Their hands in innocent blood; that mattered not;
Such things are trifles to your grim fanatic.
But they must not be tainted by the touch
Of Romans! O my Lucius, how the gods,
If any gods there be, must laugh at us
Who hold them bound by such nice ceremony,
And free from conscience—Would I were a god!

I found my prisoner was the Prophet, Jesus,
Whom I had sometime heard of as a kind
Of Hebrew Stoic, like our Seneca,
But practising as well as preaching that
Hard and high doctrine. Certain words of his

Had reached me now and then, like thistledown
Blown i' th' air, which had the ring in them
Of true philosophy: but other some
Were dreamy; part, good coin, and part too fine
A metal for this world to traffic in.
I'd heard too that he had the singular art
Of healing men by faith, imagination,—
Whate'er it be—which filled their minds with wonder,
So that some deemed a god had come to earth.
Half curiously I scanned him. Homely clad,
Like those his fellow workmen; broken, too,
By toil and travel and poverty and sorrow,
And all unlike the Immortals, as our Poets
Conceive them, and our sculptors fashion them.
Yet there was something in his look and bearing
That overawed me. As I looked on him,
There rose in me a memory of my mother
White as a lily and sweet, and of the days
When I was like a white bud on her bosom,

That now am so bedraggled. What could it mean?
Those women of the Court who rave about him
Cry up his beauty; but whom they admire
They clothe with loveliness, and Socrates
Himself should walk in guise of bright Apollo,
Not like a Satyr, were he but their hero.
And this man's beauty, if beautiful he were,
Was not like th' young Augustus. This, at least,
I could have sworn, that he was innocent,
Whate'er these Jews might say. But here was I
In this mad tragi-comedy of life
Playing the part of Judge, while he stood there
To plead with me for life!—But that he did not.
No, not so much as one word did he utter
To win our grace, but looked me in the face,
Silently searching me, as who should say,
"Thou, my Judge, Thou!" until I quailed before him,
Feeling the mockery of justice, where
The power was mine, the righteousness was his.

But how to save him, guiltless, from their guile?
So I went forth, and asked them:

"What have ye
Against this man?" He called himself a King,
And they would have no king but only Cæsar.
The lying rogues had plotted against Cæsar,
Raised tumults, broke into rebellions, cursed
His Prætors, Publicans, and legionaries,
And at that very hour were scheming treasons:
Yet they would have no king but only Cæsar!
I could not hide my scorn. Since when had they
Become so loyal to the imperial throne?
So deep devoted to the power they cursed
At all their feasts? Thereon they clenched their
    teeth,
And muttered something about blasphemy,
And making himself God. Therefore I bade them
Take him away, and judge him by their law—
They had no power o'er life—because our law

Held it no crime for one to be a god;
Cæsar was one, so were the great twin-brethren,
And Hercules, and other mighty men.
I had no jurisdiction o'er the gods,
And this man might be one of them, for aught
I knew or cared. Then rose a yell of rage,
Deep-throated, fierce, malignant, from the pit
Of Acheron; "Thou art not Cæsar's friend,
If thou let this man go."

       So I went back,
Knowing that I had raised a storm might dash me
A broken wreck at Annas' feet. And there
He stood, this King o' th' Jews, bent low and bound,
Yet with that lofty, overawing look
Which made my eyes droop—Majesty uncrowned
Of noble manhood, not yet stained by falls
In the arena.

    "Art thou, then, a King?"
But not a syllable he answered, only

Gazed on me with a look of pity. It was
A foolish question; for of course I knew,
Not for such crime had Annas brought him here,
Who would have prayed and sacrificed and poured
The consecrating oil on any head
That in brief triumph had been lifted up
Against great Cæsar. Oh, I know the man.
Nothing were less a crime among these Jews
Than treason against Rome. I've had to crush
A score of their rebellions, and this Annas
Was in them all, although his hand was hidden;
Chief plotter he of all. A foolish question!
Better if I had frankly asked him, why
Do these your countrymen so hate you that
They do accuse you falsely? But somehow,
Seeing that broken, poor, and pitiful
Rival of Cæsar, I must say to him:
"A King, then, are you?" He despised me for it,
And held his peace, which partly fretted me,

And partly my own sense of being wrong,
So that I said: "Dost thou not know that I
Have power to take thy life?" But calmly he:
"Thou hast no power, but as 'tis given to thee;
So much the more their guilt who brought me here."
What could he mean? These Jews are cunning dogs;
Of course, I had no power but what I got
From Cæsar. What, if Annas meant to drive me
To stretch my large commission till it rent?
I must be wary.
    Just then came a note,
Sent by my wife, and bidding me take heed,
Nor harm this man. She had some dream about him,
And dreams are from the gods. Pshaw! let the women
See to their own affairs, not meddle with
The course of justice. No doubt, Chusa's wife—
She's wild about this prophet—came to her,

And they between them had conspired to stay
The law by this device. I'd half a mind
To do the very thing they wished me not,
Just for their meddling; but thought better of it.
My wife has a sharp tongue.

      Then I went forth
Once more to face these Jews: "I find no fault
Worthy of death, by our law, or of bonds
In this your King, or God, or whatsoe'er
The poor man calls himself. So, I will scourge him,
And let him go"—though why he should be scourged
'Twere hard to tell, except to humour those
Who should have had the scourge on their own
  backs
Laid roundly; but a man who is accused,
We come to think has reason to be thankful,
If he escape with scourging. Anyhow,
More bitterly malignant than before,
The mob of smiths and cobblers roared at me,

And my weak plan. My nerves had been unstrung,
I tell you, or I had not heeded them.
Pilate was never coward.

      Then some one said
Something about the Nazarene, whereat
I grasped as any drowning man. "He is
A Galilean then, King Herod's subject,
And Herod is in town to keep the feast;
'Tis his affair: A letter shall be writ;
A guard ho! take him to the king; let Herod
Settle this business. It is none of mine."
A happy thought that! Herod had been cool
Of late, or worse than cool; and this would please
The old fox's vanity, delivering me
From the so tangled hank, and let me break
My fast in peace.—I saw the meal laid out
In tempting grapes, and dates, and figs, and melons,
And old Falernian, and I longed to grasp
The silver cup and quaff it.—Laughing, then,

At this rare stroke, I hurried them away,
But scarce came from the bath refreshed, when lo!
The wave rolled back. Herod had been well pleased
With our sweet courtesy, but could not think
Of meddling with the Imperial jurisdiction
In treasonable affairs; so sent the man,
After some rough and ribald jesting, back,
Robed in a mockery of regal purple,
And crowned with thorns. O irony of Fate!
Whom even the gods escape not: what fell spite
Led thee to bind this burden now on me?
I was a fool to look for any help
From Herod. He not long ago had killed
Another of their prophets—a brave man,
And eloquent, and true. I heard him preach
At the King's Court once, and he made us all
Willing, for half an hour at least, to strip
Our purple and fine linen off, and send
The banquet, getting ready, to feed the poor.

And since that deed, his conscience pricking him,
The crafty Idumean had turned coward,
And thought this Jesus might be John come back
From Hades to amaze his murderer,
And haunt him.
      As I turned to Jesus now
Weary he looked and broken, as a man
Done with the world; and half in pity I said,
"So thou art come back crowned? A king then
 truly?"
"Thou say'st," he answered; "Yea, I am a king;
Only my kingdom is not of this world,
But therefore am I come, to witness of
The truth, and who are of the truth hear me."
"Truth! what is truth?" I asked. "Where is it?
 Can
I see, or touch, or taste, or smell it?" Was
This man a dreamer, being no longer boy,
But wearing beard unblemished, that he spake

Of truth as of his kingdom where he reigned
Supreme?—an airy realm, ungrudged, I ween,
By Cæsar! We were youths, my Lucius, once,
And wasted many a night in barren talk
About the truth; when in the Agora
We breathed the air that Plato used to breathe
While Athens still was Queen, and wore her crown
With majesty; but, since we came to manhood,
We've had to act, not dream. Nor did this man
Look like a dreamer; and I must admit
These Jews, whate'er they be, are not like some
Of those strange Eastern peoples whom I've seen,
Squatting for years in some uneasy posture,
Fed on a lettuce or a stalk of garlic,
Talking of truth, and dreaming in the sun
That blistered them by day, and in the moon
That all the night bedewed them, being held
Divinely wise because most mad. The Jew
Is shrewd, and has a bottom of good sense

Beneath his superstitions, like the stones
And gravel over which a river runs.
He trades, and lends on usury, and gains
Shekels where you'd scarce find an obolus;
Keen at a bargain, hard as any flint,
And nowise given to dreaming. Yet this man
Could speak of truth, and of a kingdom there!
"Truth—what is truth?" So I went forth again.

"I find no fault in this man. He has broken
No law of Cæsar's, nor may Cæsar dread
His schemes, or be he Prophet, King, or God.
But you've a custom, good or bad—most part
Bad I should say, or only good for rogues—
To get release of some offender now
At Pascha. There's Barabbas, thief and rebel
And murderer too, him take and crucify,
This Christ I will have scourged, and let him go."

So I had done my utmost, tried all ways
To save him though he uttered not a word,
Nor sought for mercy, nor encouraged me
In my endeavours, nor approved my deed.
What happened then? A growl of sullen wrath,
Low murmur of petition unto Cæsar:
"Not this man, but Barabbas! Crucify,
Crucify this one, or"—I saw the old Priest
Writing upon his tablets, with a cold
Clear eye, and half a smile upon the thin
And bloodless lips of him. What could I do?
He knew of last night's frolic, and other things
I need not name, which might look bad in Rome
Even to one's friends, and worse when told by those
Who hungered for my post—they would not be
So eager if they knew it. It was hard
To do, for he had interested me;
But yet if I should free him, they would rend
The man in pieces, such was their fierce temper;

And if he died now, while his dreams had still
The sweet breath of young innocence, better so
Than after that bad schooling he will get
Among this people; like enough at heart
He was a traitor also—all Jews are—
And only got his due; but that thought called
A blush up in my soul, for secretly
I knew it was a lie. At any rate,
If one must die, 'twere better he than I,
And for a little more or less of blood
Upon my hands, that did not trouble me,
Although I washed them there before the mob
In token of my innocence, while they
Cried, "Yea, his blood on us and on our children!"
The thing was done so, not to be undone:
I wish it were to do, and my head cool
As it is now; no matter, it is done.
There was not one to say a word for him;
He was alone, not backed by any man,

And yet he had for years been healing them,
I wot not by what power, only the fact
Was clear, however fancy coloured it.
Their deaf and dumb, their lepers and their blind,
Their fevered and bed-ridden had been cured,
And some averred their very dead been raised
By him; but that, of course, was all a dream
Of fond imagination, or, it may be,
A trick to catch their faith: at any rate,
The land was ringing with his mighty deeds,
And yet there came not one to speak for him.
Had any man stood up and said to me,
"Lo! I was blind, and now I see," or "I
Was mad, and am in my right mind again,"
Or "I was cripple, and behold I walk,
And this man did it," then it would have been
A case to send to Cæsar for decision,
Being past my wits, and needing a divine

Insight like his. But no! these grateful Jews
Said nought but, "Crucify him! Crucify!"

They say that he died sweetly, and they talk
About his having risen again, and spoken
To certain of his followers, and the priests
Would have these stories silenced by the law.
Nay, let the poor fools have such comfort as
They find in these fond dreams. I know he's dead.
My fellows never leave their work half done;
Their lives should answer for it, if they did.
No doubt, he's dead; a spear-thrust in the heart
Made sure of that; he'll trouble us no more.
'Tis a strange thirst these priests have still for blood;
If they had shed as much of it as we,
They'd hate the smell of it. And yet I'd give
Something to learn if Annas' blood is like
What flows in other men. I hear them shouting
"The Lord is risen indeed!" I wish he were;

'Twould take a load off me to see Him living,
And what I did, undone. But that's past hope;
The dead are dead for ever.
                              Speak well of me,
My Lucius, to Sylvia and Nerissa,
What time you sup in the old tavern by
The Pincian, and the wine and mirth are free.
Cæsar will hardly trouble himself about
This prophet's death, since it has pleased the Jews,
But you might say a good word for him truly,
And strike that old rogue, Annas. A good deed!
O that I could but squeeze from these hard Jews
Some certain talents, and get back to Rome!
But they have sucked me rather, leaving only
The dry rind o' the orange. Fare thee well!

A Pulpiteer.

Sat in his inn after breakfast a lean little man with the look,
Withered and shrunk, of one whose moisture was dried, like a brook
Where the sun burns hot in the tropics; but now he was home once more
In the place where he first drew breath near the sands of the North Sea shore:
And he held in his hand a "poster," big-lettered in black and red,
Which he read with a cynical sneer; then low to himself he said:

"Service begins at eleven, but the door will be open at ten:"
That means a crush to get in, with screaming of women, and men
Barely just kept from swearing by dread of the Sabbath day,
And swearing the more in their hearts, it were better for women to stay
At home, and see to their children, instead of losing their wits
Crushed in a trampling crowd, till they go off in fainting fits.

No, I'll not face it. How should I sit still in a narrow pew
For an hour, with my legs a-cramp, and with nothing on earth to do
But stare at the white-washed walls, and gasp for a mouthful of air,

And smell the hot peppermint breaths, and the oil in the young buck's hair,
And watch how faces grow purple, and bald heads are smoking like censers?
Nay, I will sit by the fire here, and read that last volume of Spencer's.
There's more in a sentence of his than in all that this fellow can say,
Though he preach for an hour by the clock." So he kicked his boots out of the way.

That was his first thought. But hardly had he reached out for his book,
And settled him down in an easy chair in the cosiest nook,
With a big cigar in his mouth, and the cloud-smoke round his head
Curling in wavy rings, when once more he looked up and said;—

"Yet we were fellows at College together, and friends too once,
This famous preacher and I, and he was not a bit of a dunce,
But fairly well up in his classics, though Logic was always his *forte;*
A rare, good hand at debate, ever prompt with a clever retort;
Not very strong in science, but skilled with his pen to write,
And making his half-dark thinking clearer than other men's light;
A smart rhetorician truly, with a ready tongue in [his head,
Though he looked so clumsy and loutish and homespun and country-bred.
He is starring it here, as I learn; has come to revive their faith,
To stir up the fire whose embers were smouldering nigh unto death

I care not much for your stars; and for starring
parsons least;
The better they are at that, they have less the
true heart of a priest.
But they say that he gave up a living to be free
to go here and there,
Where a boat was wrecked, or the Devil broke
loose at a rural Fair,
Or where the state of religion needed a trumpet
blast
To rouse them up from the sleep into which their
souls had been cast
By the abundance of bread.—A queer sort of life
no doubt;
But everyone to his taste.—So, freely he goes about,
And passes now for a great man. That means
not much, I allow;
Once great men took to the Church, but they are
somewhat scarce there now—

One-eyed men among blind folk. Still he is followed by throngs,
And speaks, they say, to the age of its duties, its rights and its wrongs; [mint
Not pulpit commonplaces—the leaden tokens they
For everyday use—but sayings newspapers are fain to print,
Eloquent, flowing periods balanced and pointed like sonnets,
And his pews are crowded with heads too, not with mere ribbons and bonnets.
That's what they tell me, at least, and they say that you even shall grin,
Now and then, at the hits which he makes when describing a popular sin.
I do not much care for humour or wit in the house of prayer;
'Tis so easy with smallest of jokes to spread ripples of laughter there:

But yes! I must go after all, and hear what the
    man has to say:
He was not a fool, and I daresay it will be as
    good as a play.
'Twill be very bad if it is not, as plays go now.
    Ah me!
How the bloom and the gloss get rubbed off
    everything here that we see!"
So he threw down his book with a grumble, and
    out of the room he strode,
Not quite in the mood for a mortal to go to the
    house of God.

A brilliant midsummer day, with a glorious sun in
    the blue,
Though clouds were massing all round it, lurid
    and sultry in hue,
And there was not a breath to stir the thirsty and
    drooping leaves,

And all the wild flowers were alive with the hum of the honey thieves,
And the larks were hurrying fast through their morning songs, as if they
Dreaded that something might mar them before high noon of the day.
There was more than a Sabbath hush in the listless fields as he passed
Leisurely into the town, whither groups were hurrying fast
By twos and threes and dozens, like rills and streams that flowed
Together at last in a river along the great high road.

It turned out all as he pictured—the crush at the narrow door,
The screaming and fainting of women—but nobody cursed or swore—

The squeeze in the strait high pews, the crowd packed close in the aisles,
The blaze of peony faces, and glimmer of ghastly smiles,
The reeking and mopping of bald heads, the coughing and taking of snuff:
Yet were they grave too, and patient. It was God's house: that was enough.

How well he remembered it all—that quaint old chapel of ease,
With its high-pitched pulpit facing the high deep galleries,
And the sounding-board overhead, and the dove with the olive branch,
And the votive ship that was hung up in memory of the launch
Of the first of the Greenland whalers that out ot the harbour sailed.

Proud was the gallant skipper of the port from which he hailed,
And the kirk where he had been christened, and the ship where he held command,
And the minister whom he reckoned the foremost in all the land:
And he modelled his ship, and hung it, hull and rigging and block—
He had married the minister's daughter—right over the gilded clock.
They were sturdy Protestants all there, yet they saw not the deadly sin
Of a votive ship in the Church, nor the evils it might bring in. [limbs
It was not like vowing candles, or hanging up waxen
In honour of healing saints, with chaunting of prayers and hymns;
And it grew to be almost sacred in all men's memories,

When ship and skipper were crushed in the ice-packed Greenland seas.

But more than the high-pitched pulpit and the dove and the olive twig,
And more than the many-sparred whaler so neat and trim in its rig,
And the great square pew where the elders spread out their long coat-tails—
It was lined with green baize, handsome, and studded with bright brass nails—
More than all to the stranger was the pew where he used to sit—
They filled it once with a household, now he knew not a face in it.
But as he looked, he saw there brothers and sisters true
All in their order duly ranged in the old Church pew;

Here at the door the father guiding his flock with a look,
Each in his Sunday raiment, each with a well-clasped book,
While the pale mother sat at the further end, and he,
The youngest, cuddled beside her, or nestled him on her knee.
Wet or dry, they must be there, morning and afternoon,
Ere the bell had ceased to tinkle, or the clerk gave out the tune;
And woe to him that came late, or who drowsily slept a wink,
Or lost a head of the sermon, or dared of his play to think,
Or fidgetted for a moment, weary of stiff constraint!
It all came back on him now, with humour and pathos blent,

And a something moist in his eye that somehow dimmed his view,
As he thought where now are they all that sat in the old church pew?
Some at the ends of the earth, some farther even than they,
Low in the quiet graves by the surf-beaten sandy bay.
Then he drew himself up, and muttered, Pshaw! why should I yield to this?
I am a man of the world, and not a sentimental miss?

I tell the tale as he told it me in the inn parlour at night,
As we sat and smoked together by a guttering candle light.

After sitting well nigh for an hour, he said, with a mind to go,

Could I only have seen my way, but the close-packed throng said No;
There was not room for an eel to wriggle itself outside,
So I shifted and shifted my legs, and a change of torture tried;
That was the most you could hope for, one side or other must be
Prickly and stinging, or cramped and dead from the foot to the knee;
At last the minister entered, a handsome fellow enough,
Not like the country lout I had known in his homespun rough,
Butterfly is not less like its caterpillar than he
Looked like the memory of him I'd carried about with me.
Then he was ruddy and strong, and now he was pale and thin—

Was it with brooding of thought, or penance endured for sin?
Spectacled too, though once he had seen like a bird of prey
That from its rock-nest watches the near and the far away;
Whiskers trimmed to a hair, and hair in a wavy curl,
While every tooth in his mouth was white as a several pearl.
He had the cleverest hands, too, alive to their finger-tips,
Could make them speak to you plainly as ever he did with his lips:
And his voice was mellow and deep, and clear and full as a bell,
And touched in the higher tones a passionate thrill and swell.
Perfect in rhetoric truly, verging on something more,

Could he only have boldly ventured, and cut right into the core;
Not much amiss with the thought too, or wrong in the argument,
Could he only have once forgotten he had to be eloquent.

He read like a man who well had conned the words that he read,
Giving the meaning clear; and his prayers were fine, they said:
Likely I am no judge, but I thought them a shade too fine;
Rhetoric is not for God, any more than are pearls for swine.
The voice, too, was more than the thought; and I asked myself sometimes, What
Can any one find there, now, for his voice to be quavering at?

But prayers, I allow, are not a kind of literature
In which I can boast any skill, or quite of my taste be sure;
Only one fancies if earth and its praise could be left out of view,
And the soul looked straight up to God—well, its words would be simple and few,
While his were many and dainty, and every one said they were fine.
Perhaps they were real: who knows? but I could not quite use them as mine.
Then he gave out his text from the Psalm: "The fool hath said in his heart,
No God!" and after a pause, with a stroke of excellent art,
Repeated the three words "Fool!—No God!" 'mid a breathless awe—
An orator's trick, of course, yet a palpable hit, one saw.

Pity he did not stop there; just that look, that tone!
Why, they were in themselves a sermon, had they
    only been left alone
To hint their many suggestions. But some men
    have a way
Of not knowing when to stop, and of unsaying
    what they say.

That would have been the effect of his eloquence
    then upon me,
Had the sermon ever been finished, which it was
    not fated to be.   [Paul,
For mainly it was but a weft of Paley and woof of
Calico-printed with anecdotes, wholly Apocryphal,
Of Shelley and Hume and Voltaire, set forth with
    manifest trick,
Clever enough in its way, of artfulest rhetoric.
Not that there were not at times touches of some-
    thing higher,

When the man's own soul broke out, with gleams of a central fire,
Through the crust of his pulpiteering; also there were some strokes
Of a grim satirical humour—they were not exactly jokes,
More like Elijah's biting scorn of the Prophets of Baal,
Or the ring of the spear of Ithuriel, smiting the steel-clasped mail
Of Satan. They were the bits of the sermon that I liked best:
I seemed to look on the devil discomfited then with a jest
Wholly sincere and natural. But that only came now and then;
And after a while I was wishing me home at mine inn again,
With that latest volume of Spencer's, and wondering what came next,

When something went crack! somewhere, as the minister quoted his text
To clench a paragraph with; and surely the gallery swayed
Forward a bit, and the startled crowd rose up dismayed.
A horrible moment that, when murderous panic appears,
That tramples on pity, and heeds not grey hairs or the tenderest years,
Nor kith nor kin nor aught but the wretched self it would save,
At the cost of its better self, from the coward-dreaded grave!
They had sprung to their feet, and stood a moment in breathless fear,
So silent that out on the roof the rain was plain to hear
Which now was heavily falling, and then there arose a scream

That curdled the blood in the heart, and I saw as it were in a dream,
Faces of men and women ghastly with terror, and all
The galleries swaying, I fancied, away from the solid wall.

But ere the fatal rush, the minister lifted high
A tremulous hand to heaven—a jewelled one, by the by—
And sang, in a loud, clear voice, one verse of a well-known psalm,[1]
Joined in by some few near, which brought back a moment's calm;
Then he cried out, "Do not fear; not a hair of your heads shall fall

---

[1] I once witnessed this expedient tried with happiest results by a famous preacher, and effectually arresting a panic which in another minute would have been followed by disastrous consequences.

If you do as I bid; for God has given me the lives of all.
Let no one stir, till I tell you the doors are opened wide,
Then silently go, while I pray that the Lord may meet with us outside."
That wrought like a spell on them; he was not like a man inspired,
Yet the people gravely and silently did as he had desired,
Slow moving along the aisles, and down by the narrow stair,
Out by the several doors, and into the open air,
In the disciplined self-command which their faith to them had given.
Meanwhile in the pulpit he kept praying for them to heaven,
Not at all "fine prayers" now, but the downright honest cry

Of a man who longed and hoped that the poor folk might not die.
I did not hurry myself, for I did not lose my head,
But when the last had vanished, I drew a long breath, and said,
"Well done, Parson and people! That was a sight to see,
And better than any preachment the man could have preached to me."
For as they stood outside, ere taking their homeward ways,
They sang to the Shepherd whose mercy had followed them all their days.

Then, when the Church was empty, straight into the vestry he went
By the door behind the pulpit, and I followed him, for I meant
Partly to compliment him on the ready wit he had shown,

Partly to claim acquaintance, as a friend in the days long gone.
But he hailed me at once by name, for mine was the one face he knew,
So he said, in the thronging crowd, as he glanced from pew to pew;
And where had I been? and had I come back to the old Home again,
After long years of wandering far in the sun and the rain?
And was he not glad to meet me, and to recall the times
When we pored over Homer and Euclid, or hammered our brains for rhymes?
It was pleasant to get such a greeting—so cordial, cheery, and frank—
Like what you may find in your banker, when your balance is good at the Bank.

I was yielding then to the kindly feeling we have for those
We have known at school or at college; and, thinking of hardish blows
And rough horse-play he had borne from some of us then, I felt
Some twinges of sharp regret, and my heart was beginning to melt,   [of self-content,
When there passed across his features a smile as
And I stayed the relenting mood, till I found out what it meant.
"Now, tell me," he said, "was that not a right smart stroke of mine,
To sing that verse of a Psalm which they all knew, line by line?
It saved some score of their lives, and will be a good thing too for me,
For the crowds will be bigger than ever wherever I happen to be.

It was quite an impromptu thought, an inspiration plain,
Like a burst of sunshine gleaming out of the clouds and rain;
A minute more, and the throng would have trampled the old and the weak,
Though I was not very much frightened—old joisting is apt to creak,
And seats will crack with a weight they have not borne for years;
But how people lose their heads, to be sure, in their panic fears!
It is lucky for me, however. Somehow, I was losing my hold
Of the folk, and my tellingest hits seemed to fall on them lifeless and cold;
And there needed much advertising—which means a heavy expense— [bath. Hence
To gather a crowd worth speaking to even on Sab-

I was thinking what could be done—it must be striking and new—
To waken their interest in the things that are right and true.
But this now will set me up quite; they will talk of it all through the week,
And I shall have congratulations, and invitations to speak
Every evening at meetings in town and village, when they
Read in the morning paper what happened in Church to-day.

I never could settle down to a mill-horse round, he said,
Of writing a weekly sermon, and visiting each sick bed,
Catechizing the children, and comforting them that mourn,

Blessing the young folk's weddings, and christening their babes when born.
I tried it, of course, for a while; but I very soon came to see,
Though it might be all right for some folk, it was not the work for me.
Would you yoke your race-horse to a plough? My calling was clearly to preach,
To put new fire in our pulpits, and rouse every heart I could reach
By the art of the Orator, skilled to move now, and now to persuade,
Leaving the task of the pastor to men of a commoner grade.
Therefore, I have to be popular, have to be followed by throngs,
And to hit at the sins of Dives, cry out at the poor man's wrongs,
And drop the hum-drum of the pulpit, and maybe to startle men's ears—

For no one would heed what I said, if I did not
 bring laughter or tears.
Does it win any souls for God? you are fain to
 know; does it make
Men's lives any purer or truer? or souls from their
 bondage break,
And walk in the freedom of Right? Who knows?
 It is ours to sow
The seed of the kingdom; and God, He only can
 make it to grow.
I leave that to Him. Now and then, in the heat
 or the hush of a crowd,
One will go off in a faint, and one will take to
 screaming aloud;
But if their lives are bettered, I wot not. In
 every fight
There are scores of bullets that miss, for one that
 kills outright. [rife;
No doubt the vanities flourish, and sins are not less

I plant and water, but man cannot quicken to
 newness of life.
Why do I yet hold on to a fruitless task? But
 is it
So fruitless, sir, after all? These folk will remember
 my visit
Here now, and talk of that Psalm, I believe, till
 the day they die.
You would wonder how many things happen to
 make them reckon that I
Am surely a chosen vessel whom it will be good
 to hear.
So, God has often sustained me, when my heart
 was faint with fear,
And made me feel that He means me still to be
 doing His work,
Dealing out bread to the hungry, and rousing a
 slumbering Kirk.

Yet I admit there are times when doubts do trouble me sore.
'Tis not like a full day's work, this preaching an hour or more, [as well
And I don't write sermons often—the old ones do
When the place is new, and it's likely there's no one there could tell
If they be old or new. Much study is hard on me, too,
And I have to be careful of health. Life is precious. But if you knew
My thoughts now and then, you would not envy this popular fame
Which musters its thousands just at the trumpet-call of my name.
For oft when I take up one of these sermons so carefully writ,
All of them yellow with use, and glance at an eloquent bit,

Meant for some passing event, which told very well
    at the time,
The pathos seems to have vanished, and it sounds
    without reason or rhyme,
And I ask myself, How will it look, when the
    reckoning comes, to say,
There, that's all the fruit of my vineyard—the
    harvest of my poor day?
Three score, more or less, of old sermons! And
    then, when my spirits were low,
I have wished I had stuck to the croft where my
    father made barley to grow
Instead of the rush and the ling. But of course,
    that was foolish, and came
Of a jaded mind, and the strong recoil of an o'er-
    tasked frame   [repent
Strained by emotional fervour. No, I can never
Choosing the grandest of missions on which the
    Apostles were sent

To preach the great gospel of peace.—I know not
    if you will care
To wait on the afternoon sermon?"
                I told him I could not be there;
But I would remember the plate—The workman
    was worthy his hire—
So we parted, never to meet, at least if I get my
    desire.

What a life that fellow must live! half knowing
    himself for the lie
That he is, like the old Roman augurs that joked
    at their craft on the sly;
But he has not even that help to relieve his troubled
    mind,
He must try to believe he believes, and therein his
    comfort find.
Hard for a small pretender to be preaching a faith
    that hates

Hypocrites more than downright sinners, and no-
 thing abates
For one's poor circumstances, but will have a man
 to play
The hero, who has not a touch of the hero to
 moisten his clay.
Yes, I am sorry for him. How well now he
 managed that job—
The singing and praying, and slow clearing out of
 the terrified mob!
I wish that I had not gone after him into the
 vestry; so
I might have believed in him now,—for it is not
 good to know   [after all.
That your very worst thoughts of men are the truest
And when you've painted a hero, 'twere best turn
 his face to the wall:
You made him, and, if you would keep him, you
 must not look closely at him,

Though, I grant you, that life feels poor when the glow and the glory grow dim.

Ah well! I gave him his hire—to put in the plate, no doubt—

But I'd give it him ten times over not to have found him out.

Ruggles, the Salvationist.

Nay, nobody converted me;
   I was not struck down by a sermon,
And brought my evil way to see,
   And on the better way determine.

I did not drop by happy chance
   Into some Bethel or "little Salem,"
To be arrested all at once,
   And get up in the pew, and tell 'em.

Nor did some precious preacher meet
   My arguments with words in season,
And bring me home in triumph sweet,
   The trophy of his cogent reason.

Good Christians did not sing nor say
    Their joyful hallelujahs o'er me,
Nor did their magazines display
    The work of grace that did restore me.

I did not feel the sin of doubt,
    Nor haunt, like daws, the church and steeple,
I did not turn me inside out
    For pleasure of the pious people.

I could not do it. Why should one,
    With open wound, be fain to show it,
And spread his heart out in the sun,
    That folk may stare, and flies may blow it?

I don't deny that some may find
    Their sure way home in such a manner;
But I was never of a mind
    To march beneath that kind of banner.'

I had not sinned the common way,
  I never was a base deceiver,
I ne'er was in a drunken fray:
  I simply was an unbeliever.

But look here; had you loved a maid,
  Sweet-natured and sweet nurtured, saintly,
Who lowly to the Father prayed,
  And told him all her troubles quaintly,

And had you set yourself to sap
  The faith by which she lived serenely,
And round her shrinking soul to wrap
  Poor rags of doubt, that clothed her meanly,

How would you feel, if one day she
  Gave back your thoughts in harder fashion,
Of saintly things made mockery,
  And fired your doubts with eager passion?

Would it not give you pause, at least,
    And make your faithless purpose falter,
If you should hear the white-robed priest
    Break out blaspheming at the altar?

Yes, you had worked for that, perhaps;
    Yet now 'tis come, you feel it shocking,
And shudder at so strange a lapse,
    As if some fiend your soul were mocking.

I had not thought how much her faith
    Had gone to make her perfect beauty,
Nor what a change would come by death
    Of that which was her soul of duty.

And I who loved her so, by way
    Of mending, marred God's fairest daughter,
Who lately on His bosom lay
    Like water-lily on its water.

She echoed now my thoughts, and I,
  The more she spake them, shrank to hear them;
She thought to pleasure me thereby,
  And made me only loathe, and fear them.

And then she sickened, and so died,
  Without a word of better cheering,
As drifting on a sunless tide,
  And in a black cloud disappearing.

O God! what horror fell on me!
  What anguish of a heart still aching,
Hidden by day that none might see,
  But when the night came, like to breaking!

I knew what Hell was then, all night
  As I lay sleepless, moaning, sighing,
And could not wish to dwell in light,
  If she were in the darkness lying.

And in that passion of grief I felt
    What shallow thoughts I had been airing,
Seeing them now like snowflakes melt
    In depths of infinite despairing.

I had deserved this;—it was right;
    A wrecker, I had served my Master,
And piled up high a blazing light
    For luring souls on to disaster.

And she whom I had loved so well,
    For whom my life I would have given,
False-beaconed by that light of Hell,
    Had lost the guiding star of Heaven.

Therefore I took my lonely way,
    Through clouds of thunder-darkness groping,
And often like one dead I lay,
    Alike unfeeling and unhoping.

Some tried to comfort me and spake
    Of healing for the chief of sinners;
Some fain my settled gloom would break,
    By bidding me to balls and dinners.

What matter whether false or true
    The word I heard from each new comer?
Their fleeces might be dank with dew,
    But mine must be as dust in summer.

In vain they reasoned with my mood,
    In vain a better hope uplifted,
On one thing only I could brood—
    The soul that into darkness drifted.

I clung unto my sharp remorse,
    And would not have its anguish lighter,
But ever as it stung me worse,
    I clasped it to my bosom tighter.

Still wrapt in dismal thought I stood,
    And from its gloom my light would borrow;
It seemed my only sign of good,
    That I could feel such bitter sorrow.

And so I took my lonely way
    In utter sadness and forsaking,
I could not hope, I could not pray,
    I could not see a dim day-breaking.

How could I for my sin atone,
    Except by suffering and dying?
How could I think of her, alone
    And wretched, with the outcast lying?

If she were there, there I must be,
    And by her side my soul must languish,
Draining her cup of misery,
    And wringing out its dregs of anguish.

I ought to die, and die in sin,
    Without a gleam of light to cheer me,
My only hope that I might win
    A place where she would still be near me.

And one night, sitting by the hearth,
    Which had no fire, but ashes only,
A wet wind wailing o'er the earth,
    Eerie and dreary, and bleak and lonely,

I thought to make an end of this,
    And know the worst that could befall me;
When, lo! I seemed to feel her kiss,
    And hear her fond voice softly call me:

"Be still, although thy heart may bleed,
    Take up thy load of life and bear it,
Christ did not come to frame a creed,
    But to reveal the Father's Spirit."

And as I heard, that message dropt
    Dewy and sweet on my heart's throbbing;
And ere its tender accents stopt
    I like a little child was sobbing.

I've not been deemed a saint since then,
    Well found in orthodox opinion,
But I have loved my fellow men,
    And o'er my thoughts held strict dominion,

And hope that somehow all is well,
    That all will one day yet be righted,
That none in hopeless darkness dwell
    Who may not yet with joy be lighted.

For God is greater than His Word,
    His love is like a flowing river,
His voice in all things good is heard,
    His Mercy doth endure for ever.

Herr Professor Kupfer-nickel.

The lecture hall was filled with youth—
　Pencil and note-book ready—some
Still, as in thoughtful search of truth,
　Some noisy as an empty drum;
Here one was bearded like a goat,
　Another was some mother's pet,
With gay cravat and dandy coat,
　And face smooth as a baby's yet.
A seed-plot this of fruitful thought,
　A graveyard, too, of hopes and schemes,
Where some shall grow, and some shall rot,
　And some shall prove but idle dreams.

I sat me down; and by and by
    Came from behind the bema, brisk,
A little man with clear blue eye,
    And giving his stiff gown a whisk,
Tripped up, and spread his lecture out
    On the low desk; then all was hushed,
As he, complacent, looked about,
    And we expectant were, and crushed.

A small, brisk man, with little head,
    But yet compact, well-shaped, and round;
And in his face there was no shade,
    And in his voice no tremulous sound;
Features well chiselled, not one blunt,
    Thin-lipped, and with a fighting air,
As keen to bear the battle's brunt,
    And nothing for his foeman care,
With scorn for all who might resist
    His confident thoughts, and daring flights

Into the realm of cloud and mist,
    To fill it with new patent lights:
An able little man, and yet
    Not able quite for what he tried,
Who had no doubt, and no regret,
    Nor haunting shadow at his side:
Unconscious of the Mystery—
    The cross-light of a higher will—
His ableness was plain to see,
    His littleness was plainer still.

So standing there, he said, "Our course
    Of scientific search has been
To purge you first without remorse
    Of cobwebs, and to sweep them clean,
And let the daylight in. But man
    Must have some faith on which to live,
Some purpose in his thoughts and plan,
    Which clearness to his world shall give.

I call it faith; but 'tis, indeed,
    Only large reason bodying forth
What lies enfolded in the seed
    We have been sowing. From the earth
We clear away the former wreck,
    And cart the rubbish out of sight,
Then straightway to our tools we take,
    To build anew, and build aright.
No soul can stay on vacancy,
    Or on mere blank negations feed,
And though we cease to bow the knee,
    We may not cease to have a Creed:
And this is how I shape to me
    The new faith from the novel seed.

"We grow from less to more; we rise
    From vital cells, by ordered schisms,
To intricate complexities
    Of fine and subtle organisms —

A tadpole now with breathing gills,
   Then lizard fit for land or lake,
And by and by an ape that skills
   The husk of milky nut to break.
And just as if great Nature kept
   Her moulds, that we might learn her ways,
And how she wrought, and never slept,
   But grew through all the years and days,
These phases of the coming race,
   These stages of the shaping Past,
We in the unborn babe may trace
   That cheers some lonely home at last.
So doth she keep her records true,
   Repeating in each life on earth
What man hath been, and how he grew
   To fulness of his higher birth.

"Why should we be ashamed to own
   Our humble kindred in the Past?

Why scorn the seedling that hath grown
    Into so great a tree at last?
Shall we not love all creatures more
    That they are of our flesh and blood,
And that our ancestors of yore
    Squatted upon the oozy mud,
Or floated, pulsing, in the sea
    Which brought forth every living thing,
Or chattered on the cocoa tree,
    And nestled where the palm-leaves spring?
For life is one and manifold,
    And all spring from the self-same roots,
And we are ripe and growing old,
    And these are but the tender shoots.

"Our Eden—'twas some moor or fen,
    Or rolling prairie at the best,
The savage haunt of savage men
    Homeless and naked, like the rest

Of Nature's products; only they
  Were creatures of a larger brain,
Fitter on earth to make their way.
  And from the earth its wealth to gain.
So, scheming brain and cunning hand
  Fashioned the flint-tool sharp and good,
And smote the wild beast on the land,
  And hewed the oak tree in the wood.
They made them snares for fish and bird,
  For hunger sharpened all their wits,
And imitating sounds they heard
  For lures—the shrewdest of their hits—
They framed at length articulate speech
  From owls and cats and wolves and rooks,
Or seamew shrilling on the beach,
  Or song-bird by the murmuring brooks.
Then from the flint one stole the fire,
  And blew the spark into a flame

Which gave him all his heart's desire,
  And shaped his path to power and fame.

" He found the wild spark in the flint,
  And tinder in the dry rush-pith,
He found that thorns would burn by dint
  Of blowing, and he was—a smith,
And wrenched the iron from the stone,
  And fused it with his subtle spark,
Or lit the lamp, when day was done,
  And made a new day in the dark.
With fire he offered sacrifice,
  When he his gods would please or thank,
And baked the flesh, and boiled the rice,
  And with the gods he ate and drank.
He worshipped it, yet made it work,
  And be his slave, and serve him well;
He did not shut it in a kirk,
  And call men to it with a bell;

But made it sail upon the sea,
   And snort along the iron road,
And weave and knit for him; and be
   The lifter of his heavy load,
Until he learned at length, that he
   Himself was Lord of all, and God.

A long and troubled way he had
   Ere thus he came to clearest light;
At times, his fancies drove him mad,
   And he was in an evil plight:
At times through swamps of pious slush
   The ague-stricken soul must wade;
Or hew a path through briar and bush
   By tangling metaphysics made;
At times his leaders led him wrong,
   Or only right a mile or twain;
But still the instinct, deep and strong,
   Unconscious brought him back again—

Back to the bellows and the fire,
    Back to the anvil and the tool,
Back to his inner heart's desire,
    And to the force that gave him rule.
They fabled he was chained to rocks,
    And tortured by the frost and ice,
And beaten by the tempest shocks
    On the sharp pointed precipice,
And torn by hungry birds of prey,
    And bleached and blanched by sun and rain,
As he in proud defiance lay
    Through days and nights of racking pain.
Yet is he lord of earth and air,
    And that high power to him was given
To reign as Master everywhere,
    By stealing of the fire from heaven.
So true .the fable which averred
    Fire made him rival of the gods,
For where the bickering flame is heard,

Man rules, and Jove supinely nods.
The Greek saw deeper than the Jew,
  In myth of high far-reaching kind
He shadowed forth the grand and true
  Discoveries of the modern mind.

Materialist? why not? Who knows
  What subtle powers of life and thought
Lie in an atom, hidden close
  To-day, but ere long to be brought,
Like music, from it by the touch
  Of the night-wind upon a string?
Words frighten fools, like ghosts, but such
  No terrors to the wise can bring.
Lo! matter is a crystal here,
  A self-made rhomb, or octagon,
And there a dewdrop, like a tear
  Wept, silent, when the day is done,
A flower, an odour in the air,

A gleam of light, blue-vaulted skies,
A rainbow arching high and fair—
Why not a thought, too, good and wise?
Why should not brain deposit thought?
They're not more alien and unlike
Than what from many a gland is got,
Or fire that from the flint we strike,
Or currents of electric force,
That acids make with metals twain.
No need to seek another source
Of thought beyond the thinking brain.
We deal with facts; there's no such thing
As spirit; that is out of date;
Molecular tremors clearly bring
The light which metaphysics hate.
Who ever saw a soul? or who
Can tell its strength or shape or size
Or weight or taste or smell or hue?
And who its parts can analyze?

Enough that we have larger brain,
　　And that we are no longer dumb,
And that the furnace burns amain,
　　And that we have a proper thumb.
And for the rest, a man must die:
　　Yet man shall live for evermore,
His growing purpose soaring high,
　　The only God he can adore
Humanity!—the noblest growth
　　Of nature, and its lord and king,
Its servant and its master both,
　　The sum and crown of everything."
Musing, I rose, as he once more
　　Tripped from the bema, looking brisk,
And as he vanished through the door
　　Giving his gown another whisk,
Self-satisfied that he had shed
　　A light that left no shadows, no
Unanswered questions in the head,
　　No aching in the heart to know,

Whence all the longing of the mind
    For more than hard material gain,
And clinging of the nobler kind
    To mysteries even of grief and pain,
That fruit in spiritual riches, far
    Transcending wealth of wine and oil,
Ingot of gold, and silver bar,
    And corn and all results of toil.
Did Shakspeare's pregnant utterance bring
    Its wealth of words from owls and cats?
Did Dante's musical pathos spring
    From squeaking of the mice and rats?
And whence the life that from the cell
    Grows up in forms so manifold?
And what, if earth whereon we dwell
    Shall be burnt up, as sages hold?
Where then the man that shall be God,
    The God that must be man alone,
When he and all whereon he trod,

And all his homes and graves are gone?
I heed not of a creed like this;
 It is too shallow even to hold
The great facts of the life that is,
 And fit them in its little mould;
And how much less its glimmering light
 Can pierce the unfathomed depths within,
Or search for us the Infinite,
 Or mysteries of death and sin!
It leaves more questions on the mind
 Than all it seems to answer clear;
And darker is the cloud behind
 From the sharp light that shineth near.
I know the life which now we live
 Is still becoming something more,
Yet must I evermore believe
 In One to love and to adore,
Who unto all did Being give,
 And Law they were created for.

A Dream.

I DREAMT a dream. I dreamt that God was dead,
    And that we all met for His burial—
Angels and men and devils—and sang or said
An awestruck requiescat o'er the head
    Of Him who was the Father of us all.

Dreams have their logic and congruities;
    Granted the starting-point, and all the rest
Flows, like our fables of the birds and trees,
In speech of reason, and the dreamer sees
    No strangeness, even when they are eeriest.

Methought all lights of heaven were quenched, yet light
There was, but coming from another sphere,
A lurid glimmer, and a ghastly sight;
And horrid moanings filled the dismal night, [near.
And there were earthquakes shuddering far and

A while we sat in silence, as the way
At funerals is, or whispered 'neath our breath,
With furtive glance, and faces hard and grey,
And silent wonder who was meet to pray
A fitting prayer at this world-darkening death.

Then Satan strode to the chief mourner's place,
Though Michael frowned, and Gabriel blocked his path,
And Moses lifted up his grand, meek face,
As on that day of shame and deep disgrace
When he the tables brake in holy wrath.

"Silence!" the tempter cried; "is this a time
　　For family quarrels? 'Tis my rightful due,
I am the eldest born. Is it a crime
That I should sorrow most for that sublime
　　First Cause whom I have grieved far more than
　　　　you?

"I am the Prodigal, 'tis true. What then?
　　Must I be always of the same wrong mind?
Is there repentance for the sons of men,
And fatted calves when they come back again,
　　And only swine's husks still for me to find?

"I have more cause for sorrow than you all
　　Who stayed at home, and did as you were
　　　　bid,
But, ever since my most unhappy fall,
I've always meant some day up here to call,
　　And be forgiven for all the ill I did.

"And now it is too late. I've often heard
   That said by some poor fool at my suggestion,
But never quite knew how his heart was stirred,
Till now; and really 'tis an ugly word,
   Sour in the mouth, and bitter of digestion.

"Your grief is not like mine. You've lost a
      friend
Who loved you, but you never vexed his heart,
As I have done. Can you not then extend
Pity for one who has some ways to mend,
   And some bad memories of a guilty Past?

" That's the worst of a day like this; they buzz
   Like wasps—these memories—and their sting is
      sore,
And like the Patriarch when he came from Uz,
They won't go back—nothing unpleasant does—
   But cling to you, and sting you more and more.

"I can't deny that I have told some lies,
    And done some things I never should have done;
But is there any who is always wise?
And I was wroth to forfeit such a prize,
    And, when you lose your temper, all is gone.

"You have believed me sometimes when I lied,
    Can't you believe me now I speak the truth?
You ought to know how hard it is for pride
To say, I'm sorry. But I wish to bide
    Once more among the old friends of my youth.

"Have you no kindness for me? Yes, I know,
    I am blunt-spoken, have not your smooth tongues,
Am out of the way of singing hymns that flow
Like rippling waters murmuring soft and low;—
    In our place we have need of all our lungs.

" You will not? You Impeccables! But you,
　　At least, who were my friends and followers
　　　　once,
Ye men of faith who now are good and true,
Though all my arts and wiles ye one time knew,
　　Ah! ye will not refuse me this last chance?

"What! not a word? you're all in the same boat,
　　And none of you believe I can repent?
Well; it is somewhat hard, and might be thought
Scarce creditable to those of you who taught
　　Some tricks to me, for which I now relent.

" But I am sorry none the less, I say,
　　For what has happened to the Great First
　　　　Cause,
Who never lost faith in the righteous way,
Nor in the Love which was His light of day
　　Where'er he walked, and Lord and Master was.

"It might be weak, but surely it was good—
   Most goodness is a trifle weak, no doubt,
Especially if longer than you should
You still persist in your so virtuous mood,
   And will not trim your sail, and veer about.

"Well; he was truly better than you all,
   For he could pity one when at the worst,
Though pity, I confess, brings comfort small
To one whose back is fairly at the wall,
   Beaten and baffled and hated and accursed.

"No matter; now my way of life is dim,
   Stupid and without interest any more.
'Twas he that kept you—cherub and seraphim—
Out of my toils, and were it not for him
   I should have trapped you daily by the score.

"There's no use for a Devil now, since He
  Is gone; 'twould be like shadow without light;
Only where light is can the shadow be,
It was his presence that occasioned me,
  And by my wrong I perfected his right.

"But now my task is done. 'Tis not worth while
  Planning and plotting for the like of you.
What gives its zest to any clever wile
Is the uncertain match of truth with guile;
  That gone, there's nothing worth one's while to do.

"The prize once sure is nothing—let it go,
  The fisher cares not for the fish he snares;
Only to find if he can master so
The cunning that contends with his, or no,
  He throws his line, and pities not nor spares.

"But you without Him! 'Tis poor sport indeed
  Gulling what comes so ready to one's hand,
Wasting fine wit where wit you do not need,
And plying arts to sow the wild rank weed,
  Which, without art, grows native in the land.

"Life will not be worth living any more,
  And for a change, what if I preached to you,
And told you to be good, and to adore
His memory whom you trembled at before?
  That would be rare sport now, and something new.

"It's not the first time that I've preached indeed,
  Very good preaching too and orthodox,
Exalting still the faith above the deed;
And how men did devour my words with greed,
  And went away, and sinned like other folks!"

He stood erect, a mocking spirit bold,
  Having no faith in aught but craft and lies,
And full of scorn that bitter was and cold,
And good and bad in like contempt did hold,
  And even himself did fitfully despise.

Then a voice cried, There shall be no more light,
  The war is ended, evil is supreme;
But I was fain to wrestle for the right,
And beaded drops of anguish dimmed my sight—
  Then I awoke, and lo! it was a dream.

I woke up, with a trembling sense of guilt
  Upon me, as if that wild dream, profane
And blasphemous, must surely have been built
Of some vile matter in my heart that dwelt,
  By some base spirit lurking in my brain.

But as I brooded on it, there appeared
    Another meaning slowly breaking through
The lurid light, and horrid sounds, and weird
Wild phantasms of my dream; and as it cleared
    Peace came to me again, and comfort grew.

I had been reading far into the night
    That "ultimate analysis of things
Can find no need of God, nor any light
Shed by the thought of Infinite wisdom and
    might
    On the large world which Law to order brings."

"No need of this hypothesis," one writ;
    And the free fancy, roving like the wind
Untrammelled, shaped my dream, and guided it
With strange, unconscious reason, and flash of
    wit
    Too daring for the common day o' th' mind.

No need of God for science! But our life
   Is more than knowledge, and hath other needs,
When sorrows come, and troubles too are rife,
Or good and evil wrestle in hot strife,
   And the heart fails, and wounded virtue bleeds.

Truly he said, though he that said it still
   Is father of all lies, that we should be
The easy victims of his crafty skill,
Were there no God to strengthen heart and will,
   And guide the soul through its perplexity.

'Tis not the making of the worlds alone
   That calls for His wise thought, and shaping hand,
To frame the atom, and compact the stone,
And breathe a mystic life through flesh and bone,
   And stretch the heavens above the solid land.

There be more lawless and rebellious powers
    Than ordered matter, which need government
And guidance more than growth of plants and
    flowers,
Even these same wayward, wilful hearts of ours,
    Deceitful, that on evil ways are bent.

And when our steps have spurned the appointed
    course
    Of duty, and sunk in miry slough of sin,
And guilty fears rush on us with the force
Of billows, who shall heal our keen remorse,
    And speaking mercy, bring back peace within?

With lightsome heart, as if it were a thing
    Too trifling to regret, one says to me,
I have no prayer to pray, no praise to sing,
Nor sacrifice nor offering do I bring,
    There is no living God, and man is free.

Ah! better to be smitten day by day—
 For there is comfort in His staff and rod—
Than wander in that mist, and lose thy way
Among the crags and chasms that grimly say,
 No need so great now as thy need of God.

Moral-Sublime.

SAKYA-MOUNIE one day saw a tiger,
  Shrunk i' the flanks, his staring rib-bones bare,
Creep from the jungle, shuddering as if rigor
  Of famine-stricken death had seized him there.

A splendid creature, but for pinching hunger, [jaws.
  With huge fore-arm, and ravenous white-toothed
Branded with beauty, when his days were younger,
  But age had somewhat blunted teeth and claws.

Then said the Buddha; "Lo! this beast ferocious,
  Devouring me, shall straight grow mild and meek,
And turn with horror from his deeds atrocious,
  His spirit gentle as his skin grows sleek.

"For now he is a fell man-eating villain,
   Watching for women going to the well,
Waiting the lonely traveller to kill in
   The quiet evening in the lonely dell.

"But I shall be a graff in his wild nature,
   To sweeten all his blood, and change his ways:
Wherefore I gladly offer the Creator
   This ransom to redeem his evil days.

"If he go on as now, he'll grow still wilder;
   In him there is no spirit of sacrifice;
But, me devouring, he will soon turn milder,
   And part with all his fierce blood-thirsty vice."

Laughing I read, half thinking that he jested,
   Though he was nowise of the jesting kind;
And to the fancy which his thought suggested
   Awhile I yielded up a willing mind.

I pictured him, then, and the jungle-tyrant,
  Who scrupled not to smite him to the ground,
And bear him off, lest haply some aspirant
  Might claim a share in that which he had found.

Tigers, of course, have solitary habits,   [strewn:
  And haunt where brown and yellow leaves are
They're not companionable beasts like rabbits,
  And much prefer to eat their meals alone.

Weak as he was, and perishing with hunger,
  I saw him, with my mind's eye, take a leap,
And, with a snort of pleasure or of anger,
  Bear off the Buddha to the nullah deep.

Did the poor victim feel the great fangs in him,
  As they tore through the jungle to his lair?
And only think, What matter, if I win him
  To pity those whom now he would not spare?

Or did he now repent, when it was plainly
   Too late to think of anything but death?
Or did he think of nothing, but was mainly
   Concerned to get a gasp of hurried breath?

The tiger had his meal—I'll not describe it;
   These creatures are not nice—then laid him down,
With good digestion slowly to imbibe it
   Into his system well from claw to crown.

But there were some odd fragments—not to harrow
   Your feelings, for your flesh might creep at this—
Them first he hid for breakfast on the morrow,
   Then stretched him out in perfect tiger-bliss.

And as he slept, he dreamed—I do not wonder,
   Sure such a meal would set one dreaming fast—
He dreamed another Buddha had fallen under
   His fangs, to be devoured too like the last.

He dreamed of crunching bones to reach the marrow,
  Of his head buried in the softer part,
Of spurting blood that shot forth like an arrow,
  And of some dainty morsels near the heart.

A horrid dream for one who had been grafted
  With a meek nature meant to sweeten him;
But he had tasted blood, and now he quaffed it
  At pleasure in a dream-world wild and grim.

And on the morrow, not to waste his treasure,
  He raked it up, and had another feast,
And then another dream, so doubling pleasure,
  As if he were a mere cud-chewing beast.

No thought had he of growing soft and tender,
  Of sparing women going to the well,
Or being the poor traveller's defender
  From other cats that in the jungle dwell.

He had no touch of Buddha's gentle spirit,
    Nor any taste of chivalry at all;
That ghastly murder seemed a deed of merit,
    To be repeated, nowise to appal.

The brute, no doubt, was hopelessly ferocious,
    To eat a Buddha full of love and ruth,
And only feel how much the deed atrocious
    Had reinforced the fierceness of his youth.

So did I picture, as my fancy willed it,
    The good man and his fruitless sacrifice—
The blood he wasted, and the brute that spilled it,
    Having no thought of virtue or of vice:

Having no wit, but just to staunch his hunger
    With juicy meat that pleased his unspoilt taste,
And gave him pleasant sleep, and made him stronger
    To hunt for prey about the jungle waste.

That was the touch too much—that tiger story—
    Which makes a caricature ridiculous,
Rubbing the tinsel pathos off and glory,
    To tickle mirthful humour born in us.

Saint Francis preaching to the birds and fishes,
    That gathered to his sermon or his crumbs,
And Buddha fain to gratify the wishes
    Of the fierce brute that from the jungle comes,

Were one an owl upon the high barn rafter
    Staring in serious gravity, or Nun
That had forsworn the wanton trick of laughter—
    Then one might read, and fail to see the fun.

But though I would behold with reverence fitting
    What sacred is to any soul on earth,
Yet this mad fooling of a mind, unwitting
    The humour of it, wakens mocking mirth.

Moral-sublime! nay, but the brain-sick dreaming
  Of mind diseased, which we could pity, indeed,
Were we not challenged to admire the seeming
  Virtue that propped up a fantastic creed.

And yet, perchance, like other tales that wander
  Down through the ages, this too has been changed;
Buddha may ne'er have thought his life to squander
  On the fierce brute that through the jungle ranged.

*But some poor scribbler, fain to exalt his merit,
  Some plodding dullard, guiltless of a jest,
Thus fondly hoped to shew the Master's spirit,
  And only his own folly well expressed.

---

* I find this incident mentioned in that beautiful poem, "The Light of Asia." But I need hardly say this description does not apply to its author, though I do wonder how a man of such fine genius could take it seriously.

So are the great and good ill understanded,
 What time their Faith a dead tradition grown,
And on the doctors and the schoolmen stranded,
 Breaks up, a wreck upon the sand and stone.

They were not fools, those men, who earth's distractions
 Left for an aim that still our spirit stirs:
Enough, to answer only for their actions,
 Not for the stories of biographers.

Mirren.

She was but a maid of all work,
    For she could not bear to see
Idle sluts about her kitchen
    Slopping tables with their tea;
And besides, she had a habit
    Of speaking out her mind
Which might not look respectful
    If another stood behind;
For she'd scold a wasteful mistress
    Very roundly to her face,
But would not let another
    Think a thought to her disgrace

She had seen her fifty winters,
    But was always trim and tight
In her printed cotton bodice,
    And her apron clean and white:
Never knew her head a bonnet,
    But a cap of muslin thin
With a bit of simple ribbon
    Tied in bows beneath her chin:
And her features, small and puckered,
    Looking tempery and tart,
Did not truly tell the secret
    Of her true and faithful heart.

All the folk that did not know her—
    And there were not many did,
For her faults were somewhat patent,
    And her virtues mainly hid—
Much disliked her prim preciseness,
    And her stiff unchanging ways,

And the tartness of her sayings,
    And the scrimpness of her praise.
But the children, whom she rated
    If their boots had soiled her floor,
Knew how fain she was to cheer them,
    When their little hearts were sore.

She had never left the city,
    Rarely seen the growing corn,
Never been a five-miles' journey
    From the spot where she was born,
Never voyaged in a steam-boat,
    Never travelled by the mail,
And nothing could persuade her
    To go jaunting on the rail.
But she knew the streets and closes,
    And the harbour and the boats,
And the kindly fishers' houses,
    And their creels and nets and floats.

And all the grand old mansions
    Where the gentry once would dwell,
With their cork-screw stairs and turrets,
    And their chambers panelled well,
And the stately Lords and Ladies
    Who had ridden from their doors,
And the fateful tragic dramas
    Oft enacted on their floors,
She could tell you stories of them,
    Till a feeling in you woke
That the nobles must have sorrows
    Not allowed to common folk.

Going weekly to the market,
    You might safely trust her care
Not to squander one half penny
    Of your thrifty monies there;
She would have the best and cheapest,
    Yet she would not chaffer long;

They might cheat a young housekeeper,
    But they feared her caustic tongue;
Nor would she for a moment
    Linger in the sun or rain;
She had gone to do her business,
    And must home to work again.

Going weekly to the kirk too,
    Be the Sunday dry or wet,
With her Bible in her kerchief,
    And her features primly set,
There she sat in tireless patience,
    Thinking less about her sin
Than about her common duties,
    And the frets she had therein,
Not unpleased that she had done them
    With some credit to herself,
And with visions of her saucepans
    All in order on their shelf.

One day she told her mistress,
    She must find another maid:
No, she had no fault to find with
    Any thing they did or said,
And she was not like the fickle
    Fools that wanted just a change,
Nor did she much rebel at
    That new-fangled kitchen range;
And she had not made her mind up
    To take a place or no;
There was nothing she was sure of,
    Only just that she must go.

Plainly there was something hidden;
    There was mystery in her look;
But she pursed her lips, and held it
    Tight as in a close-sealed book.
They wist not, when she left them,
    What had wiled her thus away,

Puzzling over it, and guessing
    Twenty different things a day;
They were angry, for they missed her,
    Nothing seeming to go smooth;
But the pathos of it touched them,
    When they came to know the truth.

She had served a gentlewoman,
    When they both were fresh and young;
They had smiled and sighed together,
    And together wept and sung.
Proud was Mirren of her mistress
    While her beauty was in bud,
Yet prouder to remember
    She was come of gentle blood,
Having Lords to her forefathers,
    With Ladies by their side,
And loves and wars to tell of,
    And tragic tales to hide.

But the lady, when her beauty
    'Gan to have a faded look,
Mated with a man beneath her,
    Which her handmaid could not brook.
Why could she not live single?
    Maidenhood was clean and sweet;
If wed she must, why pick him
    From the gutter on the street?
She had never served but gentles,
    And she trowed she never would,
So they quarrelled, and they parted,
    Both of them in angry mood.

So the lady had her wedding,
    Though a stranger dressed her hair,
And a hand she had not proven
    Robed her in her garments fair.
But the marriage-bed was barren,
    And the wedded life was shame,

For he wasted all her substance,
  And he soiled a noble name;
Till friendless and forsaken,
  With a hot and fevered eye,
In weariness and sickness
  She prayed that she might die.

But as she sat despairing
  The door was opened wide,
Then closed again in silence,
  And one stood by her side,
As of old so trim and tidy,
  As of old with bodice bright,
With the dainty cap of muslin,
  And the apron clean and white;
As of old so peppery tempered,
  As of old so prim and tart;
But also underneath it
  Lay the old, true, faithful heart.

And she pushed a bag of something
　　Right into the lady's hand,
Saying, "Not a word, Miss Elsie,
　　It is by the Lord's command;
I've been toiling, scrimping, saving,
　　Till my bones and joints would ache,
And I've put my soul in peril
　　All for filthy lucre's sake.
Save me now from that temptation,
　　Give my soul a chance of life,
For I've just been self-deceiving,
　　Though I have been no man's wife.

"Now get you to the parlour,
　　This is not the place for you,
I am mistress of my kitchen,
　　And I have my work to do;
Take your seat beside the window;
　　There you'll see the breezy bay,

And the brown sails of the fishers
    Dipping in the white sea-spray,
And the children pulling sea-weed,
    And the old men gathering bait,
And lads the old boats mending
    That are in a leaky state,
And the lighthouse on the skerry,
    And the red lamp on the pier,
And the lass that's always waiting
    For the ship that comes not here.

Oh, you'll never weary watching
    The ships that come and go,
Or to hear the sailors singing
    As they turn the capstan slow;
Some are bound for far Archangel,
    Some for Greenland's snow and ice,
Some, it's likely, for a harbour
    In the land of Paradise.

But the hand of God is o'er them,
   And behind them and before,
And the gate of Heaven as near them
   On the sea as on the shore.

"O my bonnie, sweet Miss Elsie,
   My blessing and my care,
You'll break my heart now, sitting
   With that look of hard despair;
Rouse ye up, there's work to do yet,
   And peace for you to win,
And the web of life is never
   Only sorrow warped with sin.
There's sunshine in the rain-cloud,
   And heat in wreaths of snow,
And God's love is in all things
   That happen here below."

So Mirren pleaded fondly,
    And her plea prevailed at last,
And they lived together loving,
    As they had done in the past.
The lady broidered garments,
    Or darned the dainty lace,
Which her handmaid washed as no one
    Could wash in all the place;
And if their fare was scanty,
    No eye was there to see,
As they held themselves aloof still
    In pride of poverty.

Trim was still the lady's raiment,
    Never seeming to grow worse,
And she never lacked the glitter
    Of a gold-piece in her purse;
And on the Bishop's visit
    She could give him rare old tea—

For of course she went to Chapel
   Duly with the Quality.
The Bishop for her lady
   Was the fitting minister;
But the Kirk was still to Mirren
   The house of God for her.

So the weeks went by in patience,
   And the Sabbaths brought their peace,
And the years sped lightly o'er them,
   Though their labours did not cease;
And in the summer mornings
   They saw the sun rise red,
And the sea a golden pavement,
   Whereon his feet might tread;
And in the winter evenings
   O'er their needles and their frames
They told most tragic stories
   Of the old-world knights and dames.

And their way of life was tranquil,
   And their thoughts were pure and sweet.
And the poor that lived beside them
   Thought the better of the street,
When the gentry came to see them,
   And the great world, in the pride
Of its carriages and horses,
   Drew the children to its side;
Though a grander world was inside
   If they had but eyes to see
The faith and love that dwelt there,
   And true-hearted piety.

A Dark Evening.

The night is darkening, and the tide is leaping
    Upon the narrow stretch of lessening shore,
Soon to engulph it, while the mists are creeping,
    And folding round behind me and before.

My world is growing small and dim and lonely,
    And its brief day of brightness closing fast,
I have for comrades ghostly shadows only,
    Whose voices are but echoes from the past.

They went before me, some in youthful pride,
    In manhood some, or noble womanhood,
And none may take their places by my side,
    Or make this life, as they did, full and good.

Much love was given me, far beyond my merit;
  And its fond service, and its tender touch,
And words and sweet caressings haunt my spirit—
  O God, that I had only loved as much!

'Tis not the love we get, but that we give,
  Which leaves glad memories for the coming years,—
Rich after-glows of sunset, and we live,
  And scarce feel any sorrow in our tears.

I've lived my life; its task of work is ended.
  And there is little more for me to do;
O that its ill done job might yet be mended!
  That I could make it loving, brave, and true!

There! wrap it up—I dare not look upon it,
  The wretched failure! put it clean away;
Nothing can mend it, nothing will atone it.—
  Bury the poor dead product of my day.

Found and Lost.

I knew him the moment he came
    Past the screen by the folding door,
Though I could not remember his name,
    Or where I had seen him before:
And me, too, he knew at a glance,
    For a light kindled up in his eye
When I stept a short step in advance,
    And greeted him as he passed by.

Yet it was not a notable face;—
    Just what you may meet any day

Note.—I had this incident from M. Lemprière, to whom it was communicated by one of the parties concerned in it.

At the hunt or the ball or the race,
   Or the club or a country seat;
Somewhat ruddy, high-featured, and full,
   With well chiselled nostrils and chin,
Eye blue, like a clear crystal pool,
   And the hair on his temples was thin.

A forgetable face in this land,
   Where so many are cast in its mould,
Nothing striking about it, or grand,
   Only handsome and manly and cold.
I was over with Soult, and had seen
   "The Duke" and "Sir Peel" and the rest,
At the time when they crowned their young Queen.
   Yet this was the face I knew best.

Each feature stood clear in my mind,
   And how in his moods it would look,
When troubled or fretful or kind,
   Or chastened by pain and rebuke.

"Twas strange how familiar I seemed
    With the trick of that face and its truth :
Was he some one of whom I had dreamed?
    Or perhaps an old friend of my youth?

But where had I seen him? and when?
    And his name, too, what could it be?
I had mixed in the world among men,
    I had travelled by land and by sea ;
Could I hope, in the vanishing throng
    Of memories fast growing dim,
To pick out this one man among
    The crowd, and identify him?

You have felt how a name or a word
    At the tip of your tongue shall appear,
And you know it so well, 'tis absurd
    That you cannot lay hold of it clear ;
So I seemed to be still on the nick
    Of finding out who he could be,

When lo! by some cozening trick
    He was gone like a shadow from me.

As I gazed after him, too, I caught
    A look 'twas not hard to divine;
It was plain that the very same thought
    Was brooding in his head as mine.
For he knit his brows hard as he cast
    A swift, searching glance now and then
At the face he had known in the past—
    But where had he seen it, and when?

Then he whispered to Soult, and I knew
    That my general told him my name;
But my name did not give him the clue
    That he wished, and he still looked the same.
I did as he did, too, and heard
    His name from the man at the door;
But it was like a strange foreign word,
    And I never had heard it before.

So we stood there apart in the throng,
  A wonder and puzzle to each,
Nor heeded the harp or the song,
  Or the hiss of their sibilant speech,
Though he chatted with Soult of the wars,
  While I waited on, silent of course—
He was a milord, and had stars,
  And I but a captain of Horse.

But he tired of this puzzling, and soon
  Had put it quite out of his head;
For I marked him keep time to a tune,
  And laugh when a good thing was said.
These Islanders are not like us;
  Quite patient of mystery they;
But a secret that fascinates thus
  We must search, till we clear it away.

I could not, then, rid me of it,
  But brooded in silence apart,

Nor laughed at their humour and wit,
  Nor praised what they showed of their Art.
They thought me a churl, no doubt,
  For my answers were not to the point;
And I thought they were talking about
  Merest nothings, and all out of joint.

Not once did he cross me again,
  I am sure, for a week and a day;
But still in the sun and the rain,
  In the season of work and of play,
He haunted me all day and night,
  And this way and that way I went
Ever groping about for the light,
  Like a hound that is seeking the scent.

I searched out my memories all,
  Went over the Past like a book,
Page by page, even dared to recall
  Things that covered my soul with rebuke—

Whom I'd gambled with, drunk with, or fought,
  Who were rivals in old love affairs,
Who was owing me money, or ought
  To be paid what I owed, unawares.

Strange things by that search were revealed,
  Old stories not good to recall,
Things that Fate, too, for ever had sealed,
  Wrongs that could not be righted at all.
Who shall ope all his cupboards, and find
  Nothing there to repent or regret,
No scraps of old writing that blind
  With tears the dim eyes that they wet?

Yet 'twas good for me so to review
  My former life, scene after scene;
It gave me some thoughts that were new,
  And revived better thoughts that had been.
If it shamed me no less, here and there,
  It set me to putting things right;

But on this one perplexing affair
  It shed not a glimmer of light.

Not a drop of his blood had I shed,
  Not a livre was he in my debt,
Not a card with him e'er had I played,
  Nor as rivals in love had we met.
I was baffled, and threw myself down
  On the close-shaven grass of their Park,
And heard the far hum of the town,
  And the clear even-song of the lark.

Then all of a sudden, when I
  With long, fruitless searching was spent,
Half-minded no longer to try,
  Lo! one unconnected event,
Which neither before nor behind
  Had linked itself on to my thought,
Broke clear as a star on my mind,
  And I knew I had found what I sought.

One moment the curtain concealed
    Every hint of the scene and the play;
Then Phew! all the stage was revealed
    In the blaze of a bright summer day;
And I knew that I had him at last,
    Knew, without any doubt, it was he—
That face in the far away Past
    That lay so long staring at me.

We had had a brisk skirmish one day
    Of outposts, when Soult was in Spain,
And wounded and bleeding I lay,
    Thinking ne'er to do battle again;
And the vultures were soaring up high,
    And the lean dogs were creeping about,
And the grey-hooded crow, hopping nigh,
    Kept watch for the life to ebb out.

I lay on the bank of a stream,
    A brooklet some yard or two wide,

That whispered to me like a dream
    As it slowly lapsed on by my side—
A dream of our beautiful France,
    With its white orchard bloom and its grain,
And the vintages gay in Provence,
    I was never to look on again.

And right on the opposite bank
    A handsome young English face
Kept gazing at me with a blank,
    Vague look from his red resting place.
"He is plainly dying," I said,
    "But gallant and stout for his years;"
For close by his side, and stark dead,
    Lay one of our brave cuirassiers.

So hour after hour there we lay,
    And looked at each other across
The brook that went trickling away,
    Slowly licking our blood from the moss;

Now we heard the loud bugle-calls clear,
    Then the noise of the fighting grew weak,
And the lean dogs came snarling up near,
    And the hooded crow whetted his beak.

And all those long hours I perused
    His features there, line upon line,
Half-conscious and dim and confused,
    As he, too, lay reading at mine;
I scanned him again and again,
    He was the one thing I could see,
And he printed himself on my brain,
    Till he seemed like a portion of me.

If I closed my eyes, still he was there
    As plain as he had been before;
If I lifted my eyelids to stare,
    He was lying there dabbled in gore.
"He is plainly dying," I thought,
    "And better for me he were dead,

Those pain-stricken features will not
    Be blotted e'er out of my head."

And never a word could we speak;
    I was lying half-choked with my blood,
Slow-gasping and fainting and weak,
    And grasping a handful of mud;
While he from the opposite brink
    Looked across, as if looking his last;
And O for some water to drink
    From the brook that went rippling past!

Then there fell, as it were, a great mist
    On my eyes, and I saw him no more,
Nor thought of him even, nor wist
    Was he living or dead, till the door
Of the guest-hall opened, and he
    Strode stately into the room,
And that face flashed out upon me
    Like a face from the shades of the tomb.

Now it all came back, and I rushed
    To his club to remind him again
Of the day when our life-blood had gushed,
    And mixed in the brooklet in Spain:
But I found he had gone, as they said
    Was his way, whither nobody knew,
Perhaps, where the icebergs are bred,
    Perhaps, to Japan or Peru.

A traveller, restless and bold,
    He would turn now his wandering feet
To seas that were frozen with cold,
    Now to plains that were blasted with heat:
He knew the Red man of the West,
    Had rid with the wild Bedaween,
And oft been the African's guest,
    Where the spoor of the lion was seen.

Yet would he come back, they averred,
    And take his old seat by the fire,

As if nothing meanwhile had occurred
   To make foolish people admire.
But I never have seen him again!
   And O to know what it could mean,
That printing of him on my brain
   Who was only once more to be seen.

We are tricked by illusory light,
   Are we mocked by realities too?
Is our life but a dream of the night
   Whose facts have no purpose in view?
So strangely my path he had crossed!
   So strongly my mind had impressed!
If he must like a shadow be lost,
   Why passed he not light as the rest?

You paint a likeness with care,
   Yet smudge it all out the next day,
For you feel that the soul was not there,
   And the soul is the man, as you say:

But what if your picture were all
    You had hoped e'er to make it, and then
You turned the face back to the wall
    Which was touching the spirits of men?

Do you grudge them the joy they have found?
    Do you mean but to mock and to spite?
Why sow the quick seed in the ground
    But to trample it next out of sight?
God or Nature, that shapes each event,
    Does he labour to quicken desire,
Just to disappoint hopes he has sent,
    Just to quench his own fresh-kindled fire?

It is dark to me, dark as the night
    That moonless and starless moves on,
With only such glimmer of light,
    As to shew the clouds brooding thereon.

And I never shall see him again,
   Or know what was meant by the look
That was printed so deep on my brain
   As we lay by the slow Spanish brook.

The Lettre de Cachet.

In the days when France snapt her old chains,
    And rose up, and swore;
"We are men, we have hearts, we have brains,
    We will slaves be no more
To king or to noble or priest,
    But all men shall be
As brothers from bondage released,
    All equal and free:"
And some stood in wonder amazed,
    Their wits of no use;
And some said the people were crazed,
    And Bedlam broke loose;

And some, in pure terror, aghast
   In troops ran away;
But some held it safer to cast
   Them into the fray;
While others took snuff with a smile,
   As they tramped through the mud,
Saying, "Time we should teach this Canaille
   By the letting of blood."
Well, the people were mad, if you will,
   In those days of hot rage,
Yet the shout of their multitudes still
   Was the pulse of the age,
And the hope of the nations around,
   Who waited on, dumb,
Thinking, "We too are fettered and bound:
   Let us see what will come."
But their kings and their nobles and priests
   Gnashed their teeth when they saw,
And screamed at their altars and feasts,

"Ho! for God and the law!
Did He not make us lords of the world,
 And these for our slaves?
Let our armies be mustered, and hurled
 On their heads like sea-waves."

In those days, then, when bold spirits ran
 From prison to prison,
They came on a squalid old man,
 Half-reft of his reason,
Who had been shut up for long years
 In a stone-vaulted cell
Wet-walled with his sweat and his tears—
 Why, no one could tell.
No record there was of his crime,
 If crime he had done;
No trial had he at the time
 When they shut out the sun
From his life, and alone there he lay,

And heard not a sound,
Save the grating of bolts once a day
In the silence profound,
Or the fall of a drop on the floor
From the roof overhead,
Though the streets might be all in a roar
To have wakened the dead;
And he dreamed, as he lay on his straw,
Of the sun and the lark,
And day followed day, and he saw
But the dusk and the dark;
For at noon it was gloaming down there,
And at evening, as death;
And still in the close, fœtid air
He was gasping for breath.—
So our shepherds took care that their flocks
Should not stray from the fold,
If stone walls and strong bars and locks
Might be trusted to hold.

But the bands of that mighty revolt
    Flung open his door,
And cried, as they shattered the bolt,
    "Thou art free, as of yore
When, a schoolboy, thy wont was to play
    By the wood and the brook,
And the trout in the ripple would play
    With the gay-feathered hook;
Or when, as a man thou would'st go
    To the tryste in the glen,
And love whispered, tender and low,
    What is dearest to men.
Come forth from thy wet-walled cell,
    Where the damp and the mould
And the dusk and the dark ever dwell
    With the cramp and the cold;
Be merry, the land now is free,
    And thy gaoler, the king,
Is where all wicked kings ought to be—
    Go dance, then, and sing."

They were rough, coarse fellows; and yet
   They were touched to the quick
By the pale, bloodless spectre that met
   Their gaze, and the sick
Wan flicker of light in his eye,
   Which had not any hope,
Nor a longing to live or to die,—
   Content just to mope,
Without converse of things unseen
   To sweeten his pain,
Or remembrance of things that had been,
   To restore hope again.

So dazed, and uncertain he crept
   From his cell and his straw,
And they marked that he trembled and wept
   When the sunlight he saw;
And blinked, bewildered and blind,
   Like an owl or a bat,

Feeling out with his lean hands to find
    What he wished to be at;
For he had not seen daylight for years,
    Only dim, pallid gleams
Through stanchions and cobwebs and tears,
    Or at night in his dreams.
And it was not a joy, but a pain
    To look on the light,
Or to see human faces again,
    Or to stand straight upright.
So, dazed and amazed, forth he went
    Through the iron-nailed gate,
All tremulous, shrinking, and bent,—
    A man out of date.

He passed through the iron-nailed door.
    For they said he was free
To do as he had done of yore,
    When the hill and the sea

And the wood and the heath and the stream
    Knew his coming so well—
Unless it was only a dream
    He had dreamt in his cell.
Was he not once a lord, and had lands,
    And a chateau somewhere,
And serfs who obeyed his commands,
    And a wife passing fair—
Too fair—or was all that again
    A dream and no more?
There were so many passed through his brain
    As he lay on the floor
'Mong the straw, and had nothing to do.
    Yea, a dream it had been,
For a king must be loyal and true
    To his peers and his queen.
Then he smote his thin palm on his brow,
    As if striving to see
What would never come clear to him now—

Best never to be!
Just a glimmer of light broke on him
  With a spasm of pain,
Then the grey look, sodden and dim.
  Settled on him again.

O the horror and terror of that
  Aimless walk up the street :
Was he sleeping or waking? and what
  At next turn should he meet?
Now his ear was jarred with the strain
  Of the wild Marseillaise ;
Then his heart was smit with the pain
  Of some wolf-hungry gaze.
And why were the workmen abroad
  In the hours of their toil?
And where were the good priests of God
  With the pyx and the oil?
And where was his light-hearted France,

And its wit-loving soul?
And who were those dames in the dance
  Of the mad Carmagnole?
And O the fell rush and the tramp
  Of the hurrying throng!
And the sights here and there by the lamp,
  As they bore him along,
Where they'd hoisted a noble perhaps,—
  As the nobles of yore
Nailed the vermin they caught in their traps
  To the big barn door,—
With maybe a priest by his side
  In his old black soutaine—
They were fain to have priests, when they died,
  So they coupled the twain.
And then, as he shuddered and stared,
  The tumbril drove past
With the victims that law had ensnared—
  Some pale and aghast,

Some gay as to wedding they rode,
    Some mocking with scorn
The crowd that was raging for blood
    Of the high and well-born.
There were matrons and maidens fair,
    Who bent their heads low;
No powder they need for their hair,
    It is white now as snow.
There were old men and boys doomed to die;
    What could it all mean?
And lo! in the distance rose high
    The black guillotine.

As they hurried him onward, at first
    He would shout like the rest,
As if some fell demon accursed
    Had got into his breast.
But at length on the skirt of the crowd
    The madness was quelled,

And his soul within him was bowed
    At the sights he beheld.
Could that be the pulse and the throb
    Of a great-thoughted age—
That hoarse, fierce yell of a mob
    In its masterless rage?
How they jostled and struggled and plashed
    Through the mire and the mud,
The frantic Unbreeched and Unwashed,
    In their craving for blood!

Once more for a moment his brain
    Had clearness and power,
And the soul of his youth came again
    In that terrible hour.
He had fain closed his eyes at the sight
    He was looking on there;
But so strong was the spell in its might
    That he could not but stare,

While he sickened to gaze on that hell
    Of the fiend and the brute,
Which was holding him fast in its spell,
    Tongue-tied there and mute.
And where were the nobles of France,
    And the knight and the squire?
And where were the sword and the lance,
    And the cord and the fire?
And where was the king and the throne
    And the order of state?
And where all the world he had known,
    And forgotten of late?
Flashed a light in his eye, and a frown
    On his forehead was plain;
Then the dull grey look settled down
    Apathetic again.

Next day he came back to his gaol,
    Looking weary and sore,

And prayed with a pitiful wail
  They would open its door.
No, he had not committed a crime;
  He had just lost his head,
And he did not belong to the time,
  And his friends were all dead.
Would they not let him back to his cell,
  And its straw and its peace?
And there for the rest he would dwell,
  Till death brought release.
"For it pains me, the glare of the light,
  And it fills me with fear,
The horrors that meet me by night,
  And the sounds that I hear.
Still the tocsin is ringing and ringing,
  And women are seen
That song of the Marseillaise singing
  Round the black guillotine;
And princes and nobles are killed

By the axe and the cord,
And orgies of darkness are held
In the courts of the Lord;
And there is not a priest to confess,
Nor a monk begging alms,
Nor a pyx for a soul in distress,
Nor a nun singing psalms.
And all in confusion is whirled,
And strangeness and fear;
And I have but one friend in the world,
And lo! he is here."
So they let him go back to his cell,
And the straw and the mat.
And his friend, who could he be? Ah! well;
The friend was a rat.

Do you mock at my story because
Thus lamely it ends,

But the man in a prison-cell has
 Small choice of his friends:
Just turns from the hard stones to aught
 That has life in it—now
To a seedling flower, chance blown, and taught
 In his window to grow;
And now to a spider whose web
 Was devouring his light,
For life clings to life in the ebb
 And dead hour of its night;
And there is a pathos where such
 Fond clinging appears,
A something human to touch
 The deep fount of tears.
So, I deem that his instinct was true
 When he turned back to that
Which was the one friend that he knew,
 Were it only a rat.

It was something that trusted in him,
Something to love,
And it shed on his darkness a dim
Feeble light from above.

A Calm.

Yesterday the wind blew high,
    Tore the Minch in tatters small,
Drove us back to dripping Skye
    Wrapped up in a black cloud-pall:
And we saw upon the strand,
    Broken boat and shattered oar,
Women wailing on the land,
    Terror stalking on the shore.
Then the fickle waters, spent,
    Stretched them out and lay supine—
Samson resting now, content
    To have wrecked the Philistine.

Rocking in a summer calm,
    Making not an inch of way,
While the air is soft as balm,
    And the hills in loch and bay
Wrap them in a purple haze
    Whereon the lingering sun doth lean,
And the clouds are all ablaze,
    And the waters catch their sheen,
Every rag of canvas spread,
    With flapping sail and creaking boom,
Pennon at the tall mast head
    Drooping like a draggled plume,
We have rolled here to and fro
    All the long, hot August day,
Till the westering sun is low,
    Making not an inch of way.

Beyond the shadow of the ship
    Keen-eyed screaming seagulls come,

A CALM.

Touch the sea with light wing-tip,
    And skim away the floating crumb:
Guillemots are calling low
    To their chicks that wander far,
And rising, flap their wings to show
    The too bold swimmers where they are;
Hungry cormorants hurry by,
    Snorts the porpoise here and there,
And not a ripple can we spy
    Stirring to the moving air.
Blue the cloudless sky o'erhead,
    Blue the waveless sea below,
Only the tide low-pulsing made
    A lazy rocking to and fro.

So basking in the purple light,
    One said, "Lo! this is heaven, indeed;
Yesterday we had the fight,
    Now we get the rest we need.

Happy creatures round us be,
    Joy is in our hearts and love,
Peace is on the earth and sea,
    Glory in the heaven above."

Gruffly then our skipper; "Stuff!
    This may be a heaven to you;
As for me I've had enough
    Of those oily waters blue.
Here have we been all the day
    Listening to that creaking spar,
While the sea-gulls fly away,
    And the dab-chicks wander far.
Let me have a good stiff breeze,
    Hear a rushing at the prow,
Now and then be shipping seas,
    Lurching in the hollow now:
Anything—a wind ahead,
    Racking cloud and driving rain—

Sooner than these waters dead,
    And watching for a breeze in vain.
Heaven! there's only one thing worse
    Than to lie here like a log;
That is not to know your course,
    Sounding in a dismal fog.
Vain to keep the helm aport,
    Vain to spread the topsail high;
Better like a porpoise snort,
    Better be a gull and fly,
Better to have flat, webbed feet,
    Bad to walk, but good to swim,
Than be drifting in the heat,
    Till the gloaming light is dim.

He who made the worlds, they say,
    When His busy work was done,
Rested on the Sabbath day,
    Till its listless hours were run.

I've been in the East, and know
    That is still the bliss they crave,
Just to lie, and let the slow
    Hours go dreaming to the grave.
Well; if that was all the heaven
    The Devil had to be happy in,
I do not wonder much that even
    By way of change he took to sin.—
There's that creaking boom again!
    How the lazy shadows float!
'Tis enough to turn one's brain
    To hear that croaking guillemot!

Spring Morning.

In the spring when the cuckoo calls
   From the shade of the fresh green leaves,
And the young lambs leap on the grass,
   And the swallows are brisk on the eaves,
And things with glittering wings
Bask in the sunshine it brings;

In the morning when glad birds sing,
   And flowers on their dewdrops close,
And the meadow is breathing its sweets
   Where the bee-loved clover grows,
And the gleams and the ripple of streams
Are like joys that come to us in dreams;

SPRING MORNING.

O the sweet, bright mornings of spring,
    With the dew and the song and the flower,
And the glad young life of the world,
    As it laughs in the glory of power,
It is good for the spirit as food,
The tender green leaf of the wood.

Ah! well that the heart, growing cold
    With the frosts of the wintry years,
Can still be made glad as of old,
    When the spring in its beauty appears,
And the light, coming forth in its might,
Drives away the sad ghosts of the night.

Orwell.

I STAND on the shore of the lake,
   Where the small wave ripples and frets:
O the land has its weeds, and the lake has its reeds,
   And the heart has its vain regrets.

Hark! how the skylarks sing,
   Far up about God's own feet,
And the click of the loom is in each little room,
   Of the long, bare village street.

Yonder the old home stands,
   With the little grey kirk behind;
There are children at play on the sunny brae,
   And their shouts come down the wind,

With the smell of the old sweet flowers
    We planted there long ago;
And the red-moss rose still buds and blows
    By the door, where it used to grow.

All of it still unchanged,
    Yet all so changed to me;
For love then was sweet, and its bliss complete,
    And there was no cloud to see.

But the light is quenched and gone
    That brightened the place of yore,
And all the suns and the shining ones
    Shall bring back that light nevermore.

Ah me! for the shore and the lake
    Where the small wave ripples and frets!
The land has its weeds, and the lake has its reeds,
    And the heart has its vain regrets.

Paul in Tarsus.

It should seem that, after his first interview with the Apostles in Jerusalem, Paul for a season returned to Tarsus, for it was there Barnabas sought for him when at last the way was clear for his great mission.

So, I have drifted back to the old home,
And now am stranded here; the tide flows past,
Bearing upon its bosom soaring hopes
And daring ventures, some to reach the haven,
And some to suffer shipwreck; but for me,
I must lie warping in the sun, who yet
Am full, as Springtide, of a living force
That tingles in me, eager to break forth
In labours manifold and fruitfulness

To the glory of His grace. I would be patient;
I tell myself a hundred times a day,
"Be still, and wait; God's time is best; when He
Has need of thee, lo! He will give the word;
Then see that thou art ready." So I try
To calm this restless heart, what time I seem
To hear far off the hum of them that watch
The runner panting onward in the race,
Or wrestler wrestling for a fading wreath;
Meanwhile, I sit with folded hands, and dream
The hours away in aching idleness,
Which eats my heart like rust.

                              What must I do,
Weary awaiting, eyed with scorn by all
The townsmen thronging in the streets and marts?
A prophet hath no honour, the Master said,
In his own country. My old schoolmates now
Will pass me with a sneer upon their lips,
Or scowl upon their brows. I heard one say,

By chance, unto his neighbour, "Lo! the man
Who found no sphere in Tarsus large enough
For his ambition! We might shoulder our packs,
And peddle among the villagers, and have
Some day a shop in the bazaar, or ship
Trading to Antioch; but he would ride
O' th' top o' th' wave in High Jerusalem.
Now see him lounging idly half the day
About the doors, or basking like a dog
In some hot patch of sunshine; a traitor too,
And faithless to the God of Abraham,
Unless the letters from the Holy City
Belie him. So his pride has got a fall."
That's how they do regard me; and they would
Be right, were I the man that once I was.
But Thou, my God, the searcher of all hearts,
Knowest that what I counted once for gain
I reckon now but loss for Him whose love
Redeemed me with His life. I blame them not;

They do but scorn the Saul whom I, too, loathe
Far more than they; but he is dead and gone.

I do not eat the bread of idleness;
I have my trade, and earn my daily wage,
Enough to live on—that is all I need,
And more would be a cumber and a snare.
But when I've done my task, and fain would read
The book o' the Law, the Prophets or the Psalms,
And gather what those treasures of the wisdom
Which is Eternal tell us of the Christ
That was to come, and has come, even Jesus
Whom the Jews killed, and whom I saw in heaven,
Then do I find my father watching me,
With sad, pathetic look in his old eyes,
And oft entreating me; "Behold, my son,
Those Christians you are fain to traffic with
In their accursed heresy and schism, [would;
Have cast you off. You might have known they

Those who are faithful to their father's God
Are faithful to their brethren, and only they;
But these self-willed, have snared you in their net,
And thrown you then away. They boast of you
In their assemblies, that they have converted
The man who was their scourge; but do they trust
    you?
Why have they found no post for you? and why
Have you no visitors, no urgent letters
Beseeching you to serve their cause? You have
Eloquence, genius, learning, gifts which they
Are greatly needing—but they need not you,
Because they do not trust you, and never will.
Will you not write Gamaliel? you were ever
His favourite scholar; it would make him glad
More than when wine and oil do most abound,
To learn that this brief madness now is past,
And you a child o' th' law again. Once more
A place among the Rabbis might be yours,

A high seat in the Synagogue, for he
Hath still the ear o' the Scribes and Pharisees.
Arise, my son, and do not waste your life
On Publicans and sinners, and foolish dreams
Of fisher folk. You need not turn again
To persecute those people: you might even
Protect them, as Gamaliel did, with pleas
Of patience, till the end o' the Lord was seen
In their confusion. Certainly they are
A pestilent sect: and O, to think that one
Born of my loins should have his part with them
Even for a day! But yet I do not love
Shedding of blood. Even Moses might have been
More pitiful to the erring, though his were times
That called for sterner treatment than our days
Of civil order. There are some good heathens
Whom I have found it easier dealing with
Than with some brethren of our Synagogue,
And hold them not accursed. But, indeed,

'Tis different when a son of Israel
Forsakes the God who brought His people of old,
By signs and wonders, from the house of bondage;
Him the law judges rightly. As for this Jesus,
Surely the High Priest justly said, ' 'Twere better
That one man die than all the people perish;'
Though, I confess, I could have wished He had not
Been crucified, nor yet that any one
Should die for mere opinion, being always
Obedient to the law. I heard him once,
When I was at the Feast, preach in the Porch
Called Beautiful; and truly what He said
Was quickening doctrine, with a ring in His words
Like the old prophets, flashing light on you,
And searching you, and humbling you, until
You felt the shame of sin, and beauty of truth
And holiness. I marvel not, my son,
That you were taken with the glamour of it,
Though it be held most deadly. We must trust

The rulers and the scribes—the unerring Law,
Not our own judgments. Say that you will write
Gamaliel now, and leave it all to him.
So might you get again both place and power,
To shield the guiltless, and maintain the cause
Of charity and peace, until the Lord
Cast forth the heathen from his heritage,
And come to reign in glory."

                       What can I do,
As day by day, and all day long, such words
Are thrust on me by one whom I must honour,
Even when he doth provoke me to that shame?
I may not give my heart vent, may not utter
The thoughts that burn in me. I've done it some-
    times,
And then he raged with curse and blasphemy
Of that so holy name; but if I'm silent
He has some drop to sweeten the bitter potion,
Something that shews his own more kindly nature,

Like that remembrance of the sermon in
The Porch o' the Temple. Am I doing right
To hold my peace, when love is hot in me
To testify for Jesus, but being fain
To save his soul from sin, I bite my tongue,
And seal my lips in silence? Lord, Thou knowest
It is not lack of faith, but that I shrink
To see my father shamed in shaming Thee.
A good, kind-hearted son of Israel,
But for his priest, who crams him with the lies
That pilgrims bring back from Jerusalem
Where lies are bred like gnats. My father's house,
All save my sister's son—a likely youth,
Who does not understand, but cleaves to me—
All, blinded by tradition of the Scribes,
Look for another Christ to come and reign,
Not by the might of love and sorrow in
The hearts of men, but by the sword of wrath
Which hath devoured too long, and sunders those

Who should be brothers. None of them will heed
My gospel, or the wonder that befel me
On the Damascus road, when He I hated
Turned hate to love, and showed me all my sin,
And gave me that grand thought of God which
    brightens
The darkness with its glory. O, 'tis sad!
But neither did His brethren Christ believe;
Enough, then, for the servant that he be
Even as his Master. But I will not cease
To pray for them, although they heed me not.
Who knows but God may give them yet to me,
As James was given to Jesus?
                              Yet that James,
Although he seemed a pillar of the Church
With John and Peter, did not help me greatly
When I took counsel with them. They were hard,
And eyed me with suspicion when I came
With Barnabas, and told the grace of God

Which found me when I sought it not. And yet
I blame them not. I had been very mad
Against the Church, and haled the saints to prison,
And stood by those who stoned the dying Stephen,
And saw his face shine like an angel's, yet
Went on my evil way; but God had mercy
Upon me, for I did it in ignorance
And unbelief. And now I marvel not
That it clung to me, shadowing my name
With taint of deep suspicion, as if I
Had cloaked me with a lie to work more harm.
Ah me! we little think how our misdeeds
Do trammel up our future, and make it hard
To do the right when we are minded right.
How could I dare to fault those holy men
Who companied with Jesus, and drank in
His spirit like the common air, that they
Shrank from a persecuting Pharisee,
And scarce could take my word for it, that I

Was a new man, nor that of Barnabas,
Who knew but what I told him? Those who have
The care o' the Churches on them needs must pick
Their steps with care.
                    And yet I asked not much;
Only their sanction to go forth among
The heathen and the dispersed of Israel,
And preach the faith of Him who died for us
That we might live in Him. There was none else
To do this work. I would not enter on
The labours of another, or reap the field
Which he had sown. But my soul burned in me
To travel on this errand, and behold
Strange lands and wonders, and to tell them
Yet stranger wonders. Often, as a youth,
I watched the wild men driving to the plain,
Through the Cilician gates, their sheep and goats,
Themselves in sheepskin and goatskin rudely clad;
And I did think that some day I should thread

The dismal pass among the clouds and rocks,
And see them in their homes, and tell them all
About the living God, who made the world,
And giveth all things richly to enjoy.
I've heard that there are cities beyond those hills,
Full of strange peoples, having customs strange,
Who worship not the gods of Greece or Rome,
Or Tyre or Babylon, and among them some
Who serve Jehovah. Fain am I to see
Those cities which awoke my boyish wonder
And love of travel, and to walk along
Their streets, and cry like Jonah; but my burden
Would be the love of God and grace of Christ.

Yet here am I in this slow eddy caught,
Eating my heart in very powerlessness,
With all my powers upon me. Surely, Lord,
Thou hast some work for me to do, some task
That might be to the glory of Thy name.

I'm not a worn out tool to throw away,
And rust among the rubbish. I am young
And strong, and eager to redeem the time
Which once I spent in service of the flesh;
But now so much the more would I devote
All that I am, or have to Thee. I know
I cannot by the duty of to-day
Atone for failure of duty yesterday;
But when the fight is raging, and I long
To play the man for Christ, must I be doomed
Just to look on? Thy ways are not as ours,
Neither Thy thoughts as our thoughts. Yet, behold,
The heathen are wholly given unto their idols,
And walk in darkness, and Thy servant asks
Only the right to take his cross, and bear it
Into the midst of them, in certain faith
Of its victorious power. I will be patient.
Thy will be done, not mine. And yet I think
It would become Thee to bring back Thy sons

From shame to glory, Lord; and I am ready
To suffer for them, if they may be healed
Of their sore plagues. But yet Thy will be done.
For Thou canst save by many or by few,
Without me or with me; I have done much evil,
And maybe am not meet to serve the Lord
Whom once I hated. So, Thy will be done.

Whose voice is that I hear, which at the door
Asks if one Saul be here? My Barnabas!
He was to seek me when a door was opened,
And now he cometh. God, I give thee thanks;
And now I live indeed.

THE END.

www.ingramcontent.com/pod-product-compliance
Lightning Source LLC
Chambersburg PA
CBHW021403230426
43666CB00006B/618